前言 *PREFACE*

英国思想家培根说过：阅读使人深刻。阅读的真正目的是获取信息，开拓视野和陶冶情操。从语言学习的角度来说，学习语言若没有大量阅读就如隔靴搔痒，因为阅读中的语言是最丰富、最灵活、最具表现力、最符合生活情景的，同时读物中的情节、故事引人入胜，进而能充分调动读者的阅读兴趣，培养读者的文学修养，至此，语言的学习水到渠成。

“麦格希中英双语阅读文库”在世界范围内选材，涉及科普、社会文化、文学名著、传奇故事、成长励志等多个系列，充分满足英语学习者课外阅读之所需，在阅读中学习英语、提高能力。

◎难度适中

本套图书充分照顾读者的英语学习阶段和水平，从读者的阅读兴趣出发，以难易适中的英语语言为立足点，选材精心、编排合理。

◎精品荟萃

本套图书注重经典阅读与实用阅读并举。既包含国内外脍炙人口、耳熟能详的美文，又包含科普、人文、故事、励志类等多学科的精彩文章。

◎功能实用

本套图书充分体现了双语阅读的功能和优势，充分考虑到读者课外阅读的方便，超出核心词表的词汇均出现在使其意义明显的语境之中，并标注释义。

鉴于编者水平有限，凡不周之处，谬误之处，皆欢迎批评教正。

我们真心地希望本套图书承载的文化知识和英语阅读的策略对提高读者的英语著作欣赏水平和英语运用能力有所裨益。

丛书编委会

麦格希 中英双语阅读文库

这真的是"第一个感恩节"吗?

世界新知馆 第2辑

麦格希中英双语阅读文库编委会●编

吉林出版集团股份有限公司

图书在版编目（CIP）数据

世界新知馆. 第2辑, 这真的是“第一个感恩节”吗？/美国麦格劳-希尔教育集团主编；麦格希中英双语阅读文库编委会编；丁辉, 孟令坤译. -- 2版. -- 长春: 吉林出版集团股份有限公司, 2018.3

（麦格希中英双语阅读文库）

书名原文: Timed Readings Plus in Social Studies Book 7

ISBN 978-7-5581-4795-1

Ⅰ. ①世… Ⅱ. ①美… ②麦… ③丁… ④孟… Ⅲ. ①英语—汉语—对照读物②社会科学—通俗读物 Ⅳ. ①H319.4：C

中国版本图书馆CIP数据核字(2018)第046553号

世界新知馆　第2辑　这真的是“第一个感恩节”吗？

编：麦格希中英双语阅读文库编委会
插　　画：齐　航　李延霞
责任编辑：朱　玲　孙琳琳
封面设计：冯冯翼
开　　本：660mm×960mm　1/16
字　　数：225千字
印　　张：10
版　　次：2018年3月第2版
印　　次：2018年3月第1次印刷

出　　版：吉林出版集团股份有限公司
发　　行：吉林出版集团外语教育有限公司
地　　址：长春市泰来街1825号
邮编：130011
电　　话：总编办：0431-86012683
发行部：0431-86012767　0431-86012826(Fax)
印　　刷：香河利华文化发展有限公司

ISBN 978-7-5581-4795-1　　定价：29.90元

Contents

Was It Really the "First Thanksgiving"?
这真的是"第一个感恩节"吗？ / 1

Benjamin Banneker: Man of Many Talents
本杰明·班纳克：一个多才多艺的人 / 4

The Education of Free Blacks in Post-Revolutionary War Boston
美国独立战争后波士顿的自由黑人的教育 / 8

Experiencing the Gold Rush
经历淘金热 / 11

Entrepreneurs of the Gold Rush
淘金热中的创业者 / 15

Lives of the Shakers
震教徒的生活 / 18

Mother Ann Lee
圣母安·李 / 22

These Walls Can Talk
这些墙会说话 / 25

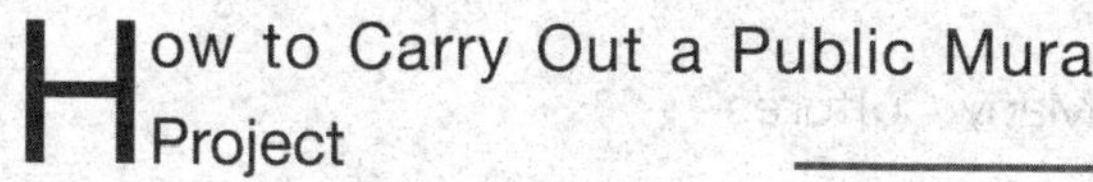
How to Carry Out a Public Mural Project
如何实施一项公共壁画项目 / 29

What Happens to Tax Dollars?
纳税人的钱去了哪儿？ / 32

How to File a Federal Income Tax Return
如何申报联邦所得税 / 36

The Battle of Britain
不列颠之战 / 39

Life During the Blitz
大轰炸期间的生活 / 43
Law and Order on the Electronic Frontier
电子领域的法律和秩序 / 46

Virginia Shea: The "Miss Manners" of the Internet
弗吉尼亚·谢伊：互联网的"礼仪小姐" / 50
Pioneers in Women's Rights
女权运动的先驱者 / 53

Educating Safe Drivers
教育司机安全驾驶 / 57
Cell Phones and Driving
手机和驾驶 / 61

Why Did the Ancient Maya Abandon Their Cities?
为什么古玛雅人遗弃他们的城市？ / 64
Remnants of the Past
过去留下的遗迹 / 68

Harvest Festivals from Many Cultures
不同文化中的丰收节 / 70
Morocco: Past and Present
摩洛哥：过去和现在 / 74

The Journeys of Ibn Battuta
伊本·巴图塔游记 / 78

“Reading” Textiles to Reveal the Past

通过“读懂”纺织品来揭示过去 / 81

Elizabeth Barber, Textile Archaeologist

伊莉莎白·芭柏，纺织物考古学家 / 85

Careers in the Museum Industry

博物馆行业中的工作 / 87

Becoming a Museum Volunteer

成为一名博物馆志愿者 / 91

The Russian Revolution of 1917

俄国1917年革命 / 94

The Theory of Communism

共产主义理论 / 98

Hands-off Policies of Calvin Coolidge

卡尔文·柯立芝的不干预政策 / 101

The Stock Market Crash of 1929

1929年股市崩盘 / 105

The Santa Fe Trail and the Opening of the Southwest

圣菲贸易通道和西南部的开放 / 107

Tejanos

特哈诺人 / 111

Let the Play Begin!

让表演开始! / 114

The Fearless Comedy of Aristophanes

阿里斯多芬尼斯的无畏的喜剧 / 118

Bicycle Use Around the World
自行车在世界范围内的使用 / 121

Military Uses of the Bicycle in World War II
二战中自行车在军事上的使用 / 125

The Conquests of Hernando Cortés
埃尔南·科尔特斯的征服 / 128

The Mexican Flag and Its Symbolism
墨西哥国旗及其象征意义 / 132

Crossing the Threshold
跨过门槛 / 135

Happy Birthday, Sweet Fifteen!
生日快乐，甜蜜的15岁 / 139

Competition for Water in the American West
美国西部水资源之争 / 141

The Designer of Los Angeles's Water Supply
洛杉矶供水系统设计者 / 145

The President's Cabinet
总统的内阁 / 148

Was It Really the "First Thanksgiving"?

English *settlers* arrived at Plymouth, Massachusetts, in December 1620. These Pilgrims had a difficult time surviving their first winter. They had arrived too late to plant crops, and they had not brought with them food *sufficient* to last until spring.

The native people, called Wampanoag, knew how to plant crops, fish, hunt, and

这真的是"第一个感恩节"吗？

1620年的12月英国移民者到达马萨诸塞州的普利茅斯。这些清教徒熬过了一段艰难的时期才在第一个冬天活下来。他们抵达普利茅斯太晚而无法种植庄稼了，并且所带的食物不足以让他们支撑到第二年春天。

被称作万帕诺亚格人的当地人知道怎样种植庄稼、捕鱼、打猎和收集

settler *n.* 移居者；殖民者

sufficient *adj.* 足够的；充分的

gather foods. They taught the English these skills. Several times each year, the Wampanoag thanked their creator god, Kiehtan, for his ***bounty***, worshipping him in ceremonies that included songs, dances, prayers, and a considerable ***feast***.

The English had their own festivals. The most common was Harvest Home, usually held near the end of September. In this celebration, fruits and vegetables were offered to thank God and to pray for a bountiful crop. Some landowners held a feast at the time of Harvest Home, giving thanks to God and the workers for their hard work.

At their first harvest time in America, the Pilgrims invited the Wampanoag to join them. ***Undoubtedly***, the two cultures shared

---

食物。他们把这些技能教给了英国人。每年万帕诺亚格人都会感谢几次造物主凯坦的慷慨，举办仪式敬拜他，在仪式上他们唱歌、跳舞、祈祷并举办盛大的宴会。

英国人有他们自己的节日。最常见的是收获节，经常在9月末庆祝。在这个节日中，人们把水果和蔬菜献给上帝，并且祈祷农作物丰收。一些土地所有者在收获节时举办宴会，感谢上帝，感谢工人们的辛勤劳动。

清教徒在美洲的第一个收获季节时邀请了万帕诺亚格人来参加他们的

---

bounty *n.* 丰富的；慷慨的　　**feast** *n.* 筵席；宴会
undoubtedly *adv.* 无疑地；无庸置疑地

their traditions. This united festival may not have been the "First Thanksgiving", however. ***Accounts*** do not say that it was a feast of thanksgiving, and both the English and the Wampanoag had long celebrated the harvest in their own ways.

庆祝活动。毫无疑问，两个文化不同的民族分享了他们的传统。但是，这次联合庆祝可能并不是"第一个感恩节"。无记载说这是一次感恩宴会，并且英国人和万帕诺亚格人都已经有他们各自庆祝丰收的悠久历史了。

account *n.* 描述；叙述

2

Benjamin Banneker: Man of Many Talents

Benjamin Banneker, scientist and inventor, was a free African American. He was born in 1731 on his family's ***tobacco*** farm near Baltimore, Maryland. His mother, Mary, was a free woman, and his father, Robert, was an ***enslaved*** African American whom Mary had bought. His grandmother, a free woman

本杰明·班纳克：一个多才多艺的人

美国科学家和发明家本杰明·班纳克是一个自由黑人。他于1731年出生于靠近马里兰州巴尔的摩市的自家烟草农场。他的母亲玛丽是一个自由人，而他的父亲罗伯特是玛丽所买的一名美国黑人奴隶。他的外祖母来自英国，是一个自由人，以前做过契约仆人，她和一个名叫

tobacco *n.* 烟叶，烟草

enslaved *adj.* 被奴役的

who was a former ***indentured*** servant from England, had married a slave named Banna Ka. That name was later changed to Bannaky and then to Banneker when Benjamin was in school.

When Banneker was growing up, public education was not readily ***available*** to African Americans. His grandmother taught him to read. Later he learned to write and studied mathematics at a Quaker school.

Banneker began to show signs of having extraordinary talent when he was still a young man. In 1753 he built the first striking clock in America. He dismantled a pocket watch to see how it worked and then built wooden copies of its parts. He even included hand-carved ***gears***. The clock kept perfect time for 40 years.

As an adult, Banneker lived in a cabin he built. He borrowed books

班纳·卡的奴隶结了婚。班纳这个名字后来变成了班纳基，然后在本杰明上学时又变成了班纳克。

在班纳克成长期间，黑人很难接受到学校教育。他的外祖母教他读书。之后他在一所贵格学校学习写作和数学。

在他年轻时，班纳克就开始显露出了其拥有非凡才能的迹象。1753年，他造出了美国第一个自鸣钟。他先是拆开一个怀表，研究其如何工作，然后加以复制造出了相应的木制零件。他甚至手工雕刻出了齿轮。这个钟准时运行达40年之久。

成年后，班纳克住在自己建造的小屋里。他从邻居那里借来书和设

indentured *adj.*（旧时）签订契约的　　**available** *adj.* 可获得的；可找到的
gear *n.* 齿轮；传动装置

and equipment from neighbors and taught himself ***astronomy*** and advanced mathematics. He even had a skylight in his cabin to help him study the skies. In 1789 Banneker predicted a solar eclipse.

Banneker put his skills to work when he published a series of ***almanacs*** in the 1790s. These almanacs included information, based on his calculations, about weather and eclipses. In 1792 he sent the manuscript for his first almanac to Secretary of State (later President) Thomas Jefferson, who had a keen interest in science. The two men began to ***correspond***. Jefferson (a slaveholder) and Banneker (the son of an enslaved African American) discussed how the abilities of African Americans and whites differed.

Perhaps Banneker's most visible ***legacy*** may be seen in the layout of Washington, D.C. In 1791 Banneker became part of the team that

---

备，自学天文学和高等数学。他的小屋甚至有一个天窗助其研究天空。1789年，班纳克预测了一次日食。

班纳克应用自己的技能于18世纪90年代出版了一系列的历书。这些历书中包括以他的计算结果为依据的有关天气和日月蚀的知识。1792年，他把其第一本历书的手稿寄给了对科学极感兴趣的时任国务卿（后来的总统）托马斯·杰弗逊。两人开始互通信件。杰弗逊（奴隶主）和班纳克（黑人奴隶的儿子）讨论了黑人和白人在能力上有何不同。

或许人们可从华盛顿特区的规划上看到班纳克最引人注目的遗产。

---

astronomy *n.* 天文学
almanac *n.* 历书；年历
correspond *v.* 通信
legacy *n.* 遗产

was designing the new capital city. American soldier and ***architect*** Pierre L'Enfant headed the project. Shortly after the initial plans were surveyed and drawn, L'Enfant left the project and took his drawings with him. To keep the project moving, Banneker re-created the team's proposed layout from memory—an amazing ***feat*** that took him only two days.

Benjamin Banneker accomplished many feats as a mathematician, an astronomer, and an inventor. He also used his reputation to push for social reforms, including ***racial*** equality and peace.

1791年，班纳克成为了新首都规划设计小组的一员。美国士兵和建筑师皮埃尔·朗方主持了这个项目。在勘测绘制最初的图纸后不久，朗方便带着他的设计图离开了。为了让项目进行下去，班纳克根据记忆重新画出规划小组所提出的设计方案——这个惊人之举只花了他两天的时间。

作为一名数学家、天文学家和发明家，本杰明·班纳克完成了许多壮举。他还利用自己的声誉去奋力争取包括种族平等与和平的社会改革。

---

architect *n.* 建筑师；设计师

feat *n.* 功绩；英勇事迹

racial *adj.* 种族的；种族间的

3

The Education of Free Blacks in Post-Revolutionary War Boston

In 1779 Thomas Jefferson first ***proposed*** a system of tax-supported public education. Although the plan failed, it became the basis for a system of public education that came about in the 1840s. Before then opportunities for schooling usually went to boys from wealthy families, funded by private or ***religious*** groups.

美国独立战争后波士顿的自由黑人的教育

1779年，托马斯·杰弗逊首次提出了一种依靠税收维持的公共教育体制。虽然该方案没能成功，但它却成了19世纪40年代出现的公共教育体制的基础。在那之前，由私人或宗教团体资助的接受学校教育的机会通常是属于那些来自富裕家庭的男孩子们。

propose *v.* 提出；提名

religious *adj.* 宗教的

Boston's free black community saw the need to take care of its children. In 1787 Prince Hall, a ***prominent*** African American, asked the state to start a school for black children. They ***denied*** both this request and later ***petitions***. Hall then opened his own school in his home in 1798. Ten years later, he moved the school to the local African Meeting House.

In the 1820s, schooling for African American children improved when authorities in Boston started two free schools for them. Then, in 1834, the first school in the country that was just for African American children was built. It was named after white businessman Abiel Smith. Smith had left $2,000 in his will for the education of black children.

波士顿的自由黑人社区觉得有必要去照看社区里的孩子。1787年，普林斯·霍尔这位著名的黑人恳求州政府为黑人儿童开办学校。这个请求以及随后的请愿都被驳回了。霍尔于是于1798年在自己家里开办了学校。十年后，他把学校搬到了当地的非洲人会堂。

19世纪20年代，波士顿当局为黑人儿童开办了两所免费学校，使他们的学校教育得到了改善。接着在1834年，美国国内第一所专为黑人儿童开设的学校建立了起来。这所学校以白人商人亚别·史密斯的名字命名。史密斯在他的遗嘱里留下2 000美元用于黑人儿童教育。

---

prominent *adj.* 重要的；著名的；杰出的

deny *v.* 否认；否定

petition *n.* 请愿书

In the late 1840s, some African American parents ***sued*** unsuccessfully to ***compel*** public schools to admit their children. The courts ruled that the parents' lawyers had not proved that the Smith School was ***inferior*** to public schools. Segregation—racial separation—was not outlawed in Massachusetts public schools until 1855.

在19世纪40年代后期，一些黑人父母发起了迫使公立学校录取他们孩子的诉讼，但没有成功。法院裁定这些父母的律师不能证明史密斯学校比公立学校差。马萨诸塞州公立学校的隔离做法——种族隔离——直到1855年才被宣布为不合法。

---

sue *v.* 控告；提出诉讼　　**compel** *v.* 强迫；迫使

inferior *adj.* 较差的；次的；比不上……的

Experiencing the Gold Rush

In 1848 a few men building a sawmill in California discovered gold. By 1849 many people, mostly men, had left their homes and *flocked* to California to search for the precious metal or set up businesses. Although most of the ***prospectors***, called forty-niners, were from the United States, some came from Mexico, Chile, China, and

经历淘金热

1848年，一些人在加利福尼亚建造一座锯木场时发现了金子。到1849年，很多人，大部分是男性，离开家涌向加利福尼亚去寻找这种贵金属或是去创业。虽然被称之为49年者的采矿者主要来自于美国，有一些人则来自墨西哥、智利、中国以及其他国

flock *v.* 群集；聚集；蜂拥

prospector *n.* 勘探者；探矿者

other countries. All of them hoped to become rich.

Many city folk who searched for gold in California were unaccustomed to ***manual*** labor. Their dreams of riches ***shattered*** when, after months or even years of hard work, they found little or no gold. Some of their letters home described the wretched working conditions they endured and their longing for loved ones. Disappointment often led to resentment of competitors, especially when those who were successful were foreigners.

Many Mexicans and Chileans had been miners before coming to California. Their knowledge and experience helped them. This, in turn, made them the target of attacks by American miners. In 1850 the California ***legislature*** approved a tax on all foreign miners.

家。他们所有人都希望发财。

来加利福尼亚寻找金子的城里人很多都不习惯干体力劳动。在数月、甚至数年的艰苦劳作后，他们几乎没发现什么金子，财富梦想就此破灭了。他们的一些家书描述了其所经受的极差的工作条件以及对所爱之人的想念。失望往往导致对竞争者的忿恨，特别是当获得成功的是那些外国人时。

很多墨西哥人和智利人在来加利福尼亚之前就当过矿工。他们的知识和经验帮助了他们。这反过来又让他们成了美国矿工的攻击对象。1850年，加利福尼亚立法机构批准对所有外国矿工征税。一些人缴纳了税金继

---

manual *adj.* 手工的；体力的

shatter *v.* （使）破碎；碎裂

legislature *n.* 立法机关

Although some paid the tax and kept searching for gold, many others left California or stopped mining.

Some of the most successful miners were Chinese ***immigrants***. Many had been farmers in China and hoped to find enough gold to pay off debts. Others had been miners. They were used to hard work—and, as they usually worked in large groups, they could work more efficiently than one person alone. They often took over ***claims*** abandoned by American miners, yet still they managed to find enough gold dust to ***eke*** out a profit.

As resentment against foreigners grew, many Chinese were beaten or their mining camps destroyed. Some returned to China.

续寻找金子，但其他很多人则离开了加利福尼亚或是不再淘金了。

最成功的矿工当中包括一部分中国移民。他们中一些人在中国时是农民，希望找到足够的金子来还清债务。其他人则曾是矿工。他们习惯于辛苦工作——并且由于通常一大群人一起工作，他们的工作效率要比独自工作的人高。他们常常接管美国矿工放弃的探矿权，然而他们仍旧成功地发现了足够的金沙来维持盈利。

随着对外国人的怨恨增加，许多中国人挨了打，或是他们的采矿营

---

immigrant *n.* （外来）移民；外侨

claim *n.* 所有权

eke *v.* 使……的供应持久

Others opened businesses. Because few women had journeyed to California, there were opportunities to do jobs that women traditionally did, such as washing clothes or cooking. Some Chinese who opened laundries or restaurants became wealthy.

African Americans also mined for gold during the Gold Rush, but not all of them were free. California had become a state in 1850 and did not allow ***slavery***, but the ***practice*** was still legal in other states. Some slaveholders brought enslaved African Americans to California to prospect for gold. Unlike other miners, some of these African Americans wanted to find gold so that they could buy freedom for themselves and their families. Some succeeded, and in the end perhaps they gained the most valuable of all riches.

地遭到摧毁。一些人返回了中国。其他人做起了生意。因很少有妇女来加利福尼亚，他们就有了大量机会去从事传统上由妇女做的工作，例如洗衣服、做饭。一些开办了洗衣店或是饭馆的中国人发了财。

在淘金热期间黑人也来淘金，但他们不是所有人都是自由人。加利福尼亚于1850年成为美国的一个州并且不允许奴隶制存在，但奴隶制在其他州仍然是合法的。一些奴隶主把黑人奴隶带到加利福尼亚来淘金。不像其他矿工，这些黑人中有一些想要找到黄金以便能为自己以及家人赎回自由。一些人做到了，也许最终他们得到了一切财富中最珍贵的东西。

---

slavery *n.* 奴隶制

practice *n.* 通常的做法；惯例

5

Entrepreneurs of the Gold Rush

During the Gold Rush, many ***entrepreneurs*** did not mine for gold, yet some became ***fabulously*** wealthy. Although James Marshall tried to keep his discovery of gold at Sutter's Mill a secret, Sam Brannan, a salesman, soon heard about it and set out to make his fortune. He bought all of the mining equipment he

淘金热中的创业者

在淘金热期间，很多创业者并不开采黄金，然而他们中一些人变得极其富有。虽然詹姆斯·马歇尔试图保守在萨特的工厂发现金子这一秘密，但萨姆·布兰南，一名销售员，不久便听到了这个消息，并着手从中发财。他把能找到的所有采矿设备都买了下来。然后他登广告

entrepreneur *n.* 创业者

fabulously *adv.* 极其；非常

could find. Then he advertised the discovery of gold. Soon people were flocking to Brannan's store to buy picks, shovels, and other mining equipment at his ***inflated*** prices. In less than three months' time, he had earned $36,000. By 1856, just eight years after Marshall had discovered gold, Brannan was the richest man in California.

Other enterprising people also took advantage of gold seekers. Parts of the overland route to California were devoid of drinkable water. Many unprepared travelers died of thirst. Entrepreneurs ***capitalized on*** the situation by selling water along the way, sometimes for as much as $100 a drink.

Similarly people charged ***outrageous*** amounts of money for things that miners needed. Some made their fortunes cooking, cleaning,

---

说发现了金子。很快人们都涌到布兰南的店里来购买价格飞涨的鹤嘴镐、铁铲和其他采矿设备。在不到三个月的时间里，他赚了36 000美元。到1856年，仅仅是马歇尔发现金子的8年之后，布兰南成了加利福尼亚最富有的人。

其他创业者同样是占了淘金者的便宜。在去加利福尼亚的陆上线路上，部分地方缺乏饮用水。很多准备不充分的旅行者死于口渴。创业者利用这种情形沿途售水，有时一杯水高达100美元。

同样，人们在向矿工出售所需之物时要价也是高得离谱。在淘金热

---

inflated *adj.* 过高的；高得不合理的

capitalize on 充分利用

outrageous *adj.* 反常的；令人惊讶的

doing laundry, running hotels, or lending money during the Gold Rush.

In 1853 Levi Strauss ***established*** a dry goods business in San Francisco. He sold ***supplies*** to miners and made a fortune. However, today he is best remembered for the jeans that his company started making after the Gold Rush.

期间一些人通过帮人做饭、打扫卫生、洗衣服、经营旅店或是放贷而发了财。

1853年，李维·斯特劳斯在旧金山开设了一家干货店。他向矿工出售日常用品发了财。然而，今天他是因其公司在淘金热后开始制作的牛仔裤而为人们所牢记。

establish *v.* 建立；创办

supply *n.* 补给；补给品

6

Lives of the Shakers

The Shakers are a religious ***sect*** that ***flourished*** in the United States between the time of the American Revolution and the first half of the nineteenth century. They were most commonly found in New York, New England, and the ***frontier*** areas of Kentucky and Ohio.

震教徒的生活

震教徒是美国独立战争时期至19世纪上半世纪这一期间兴盛于美国的一个宗教派别。他们最常见于纽约、新英格兰地区以及肯塔基州和俄亥俄州的边远地区。

sect *n.* 派别；宗派

flourish *v.* 繁荣；昌盛

frontier *n.* 开发地区边缘地带；边远地区

The Shakers have been described as ***millenarian*** because of their belief that Christ's Second Coming would usher in 1,000 years of peace. They were first known as the Shaking Quakers. The name came about as a result of the extreme trembling that they exhibited during their ***ecstatic*** dancing and singing in their worship services.

Shakers followed an extremely simple communal lifestyle. They held all property in common. Men and women shared equally in the work and ***governance*** of the community. The spare design of their buildings and furniture, their old-fashioned clothing, and their unfashionable hairstyles reflected their emphasis on the spiritual rather than the material.

The community was organized into families. A Shaker family was larger than a typical ***nuclear family***. Elders, deacons, and trustees,

---

由于笃信基督的再临将迎来千年和平，震教徒被描绘成是千禧年信徒。起初，他们被称为抖动的贵格会教徒。这个名字产生的原因是他们在礼拜仪式上欣喜若狂的舞蹈和歌唱中所表现出的极端抖动。

震教徒遵循一种极其简单的集体生活方式。他们共同拥有财产。男女在工作和社区管理中地位平等。他们简洁的建筑和家具设计、老式的服装和不时髦的发型反映了他们重视精神方面而非物质方面。

社区由家庭组成。一个震教徒家庭比一个典型的核心家庭要大。老人、执事和受托人，无论男女，是每个家庭的首领。每个家庭都有自己的

---

millenarian *n.* 千禧年信徒
ecstatic *adj.* 狂喜的；热情极高的
governance *n.* 统治；管理
nuclear family 核心家庭；小家庭

both male and female, were the heads of each family. Each family had its own dormitory, cooking and eating areas, barns, and work areas. Younger members might be engaged in outdoor or indoor tasks, depending on their abilities as farmers or ***artisans***. Older members and those who had previously been married were most likely to be ***engaged*** in the business aspects of the community.

The main belief that distinguished Shakers from mainstream Protestants was their practice of ***celibacy***. Men and women lived in separate dormitories. The Shaker sect grew by ***converting*** adults and rearing orphans. As adults the orphans could choose whether to stay with the community.

Hard work was as important in the Shakers' relationship to God as were formal worship services. The Shakers engaged in farming

---

宿舍、做饭和用餐的地方、谷仓和工作区域。年轻成员可从事室内或室外工作，这取决于他们是农民还是工匠。年老成员和那些之前结过婚的人最有可能参与社区的商业方面事宜。

震教徒与主流新教的主要信仰区别在于前者的独身做法。这个教的男人和女人分开来住。它通过让成人皈依和抚养孤儿来发展自己。孤儿长大成人后可选择是否和社区住在一起。

在震教徒与上帝的关系中，努力工作与正式的礼拜仪式一样重要。震教徒从事农业以及牧羊、养蜂等相关活动。他们还制造简单家具和手工艺

---

artisan *n.* 工匠；技工
celibacy *n.* 独身
engage *v.* 从事；使参加
convert *v.* 使转变；皈依；改变信仰

and related activities such as sheep herding and raising bees. They also made simple furniture and craft items for sale. They used the proceeds to buy land.

Although many people admired their prosperous farms, functional furniture, and simple building style, the Shakers' ecstatic worship and their practice of holding ***seances*** aroused suspicion among mainstream Christians. Shakers reached the peak of their membership (about 6,000) right before the Civil War. After that, their membership ***declined***, and after 1965 they accepted no new members. Today only a few elderly women live in a Shaker community in Maine.

品用来出售。他们用这些收入购买土地。

尽管很多人羡慕他们富裕的农场、实用的家具和简洁的建筑风格，震教徒的狂喜的礼拜和举办降神会的做法在主流基督教徒中引起怀疑。震教徒的信徒人数在内战之前达到顶峰（大约六千人）。在那以后，它的信徒人数下降，在1965年之后便没有新信徒加入了。今天只有几个上了年纪的妇女还在缅因州的一个震教徒社区居住着。

seance *n.* 降神会（设法和亡灵说话）　　**decline** *v.* 减少；下降

7

Mother Ann Lee

Ann Lee was born in Manchester, England, in 1736. A poor, ***illiterate*** young textile worker, she married a ***blacksmith*** and had four children, all of whom died young. From an early age, Lee exhibited great ***piety***; at the age of 22, she joined a new religious group known as the Shaking Quakers. While in prison for

圣母安·李

1736年，安·李在英格兰的曼切斯特出生。她是个年轻的纺织工人，人很穷，没受过教育，嫁给了一个铁匠并生了四个孩子，但都夭折了。李从小就很虔诚；22岁时，她加入了一个叫做抖动的贵格会的新宗教团体。在因遵循自己的宗教习俗而入狱时，

---

illiterate *adj.* 文盲的；没受教育的

blacksmith *n.* 铁匠

piety *n.* 虔诚

observing her religious practices, she experienced spiritual ***visions*** and ***trances***. She became convinced that she was Christ, whose Second Coming had been foretold, in female form. A small group of followers, including her husband, acknowledged her as their leader in 1772 and began to refer to her as Mother Ann.

One of Mother Ann's visions led her to escape further ***persecution*** by coming to the United States. In 1776, near Albany, New York, Mother Ann and her followers established the first Shaker farming community. Mother Ann's husband had by this time abandoned her. Perhaps as a result of this experience and the early deaths of her children, Mother Ann preached the doctrine of celibacy. Being

---

她经历了精神幻象和催眠。她确信自己就是那个预言中的以女性身份再临人间的基督。包括她丈夫在内的一小群追随者于1772年承认她是他们的领导者，并开始称她为圣母安·李。

圣母安的一个幻象导致她来美国逃避更多的迫害。1776年，在纽约州的奥尔巴尼市附近圣母安和她的追随者创建了首个震教徒农业社区。那时她的丈夫已经抛弃了她。可能是因为这次经历以及孩子的夭折，圣母安

---

vision *n.* 想象；幻觉　　**trance** *n.* 催眠状态；昏睡状态

persecution *n.* （尤指宗教、政治信仰或种族而遭受的）迫害

charismatic, she attracted converts from other congregations, many of whom had experienced ***conversion*** but were unsure how to put their faith to work.

Mother Ann Lee died in 1784, but the Shaker communities continued to grow for almost 80 years. Her personal writings are known as Mother's Wisdom.

宣扬独身教义。她魅力非凡，吸引了来自其他宗教会众的皈依者，这些人中大多数都经历了皈依过程但却不确定如何去实践信仰。

圣母安·李于1784年离世，但震教徒社区继续发展了差不多八十年的时间。她的个人著作被称作圣母的智慧。

---

charismatic *adj.* 有魅力的

conversion *n.* 皈依

8

These Walls Can Talk

Human beings have been painting *murals* on walls since they first started making art. Murals have been used to illustrate history and memorialize important people. In modern times, some murals in public locations have *stirred up controversy*.

Our prehistoric ancestors produced the

这些墙会说话

从刚开始创造艺术时起，人类就一直在墙上绘制壁画了。壁画被用来诠释历史、纪念重要人物。在当今，一些位于公共场所的壁画引起了争议。

在大约30 000年以前的旧石器时代，即石器时代早期，我们的史前祖

mural *n.* 壁画

controversy *n.* 争论；论战

stir up 激起；煽动；唤起

first-known wall paintings during the Paleolithic Period, the early Stone Age, some 30,000 years ago. Some of these murals, found deep inside caves at Lascaux, France, feature images of horses, bison, deer, mammoths, and other animals. ***Anthropologists*** believe that the murals may have been used in rituals. One possibility is that they served as requests to the gods for good hunting.

The ancient Egyptians decorated the walls of their ***tombs*** with paintings. These often showed activities of daily life, such as hunting and farming. One famous scene shows musicians and dancers at a great feast. During the Italian Renaissance, painters decorated walls with paintings called ***frescoes***. In a church, frescoes might depict biblical stories. In private homes, they might portray family members and important events.

先创作出了已知的最早的壁画。其中一些在法国拉斯科洞穴深处发现的壁画以马、野牛、鹿、猛犸象以及其他动物的形象为主。人类学家相信壁画可能用于宗教仪式。一种可能是他们用于祈求神灵保佑狩猎顺利。

古埃及人用绘画来装饰墓室的墙壁。这些绘画常常展示了日常生活，如狩猎、农耕。其中一个著名的场景展示了宴会上的乐师和舞蹈者。在意大利文艺复兴时期，画家用叫做湿壁画的绘画来装饰墙壁。在教堂，湿壁画可描绘圣经故事。在私人家里，它们可描绘家庭成员和重要事件。

---

anthropologist *n.* 人类学家；人类学者　　**tomb** *n.* 坟墓（尤指地面以上的部分）
fresco *n.* 湿壁画

Many artists in the twentieth and twenty-first centuries have used murals to ***promote*** social change. In the 1920s, the Mexican government hired artists such as Diego Rivera and José Orozco to create large public murals illustrating Mexican history and promoting the ideals of the revolution of 1917. These artists also created murals in the United States that expressed their beliefs.

The mural tradition ***caught on*** among the Hispanic groups in the Southwest. Today, Los Angeles is a center for mural art. The Great Wall of Los Angeles, the world's longest mural, ***stretches*** more than 2,500 feet. This mural took six years to paint and involved more than 200 young people working under the direction of muralist Judy Baca. The mural illustrates California history.

在20世纪和21世纪，许多艺术家用壁画来推动社会变革。20世纪20年代，墨西哥政府雇用迭戈·里维拉和何塞·奥罗斯科等艺术家来创造大型的公共壁画，诠释墨西哥历史、宣扬1917年革命理想。这些艺术家还在美国创作了壁画表达他们的信仰。

这种壁画传统在美国西南部讲西班牙语的群体中流行起来。今天，洛杉矶是壁画艺术中心。洛杉矶大墙——世界最长的壁画，绵延2 500多英尺长。这个壁画花了6年的时间来绘制，有200多名年轻人在壁画家朱迪·贝卡的指导下参与其中。这个壁画诠释了加利福尼亚的历史。

---

promote *v.* 促进；提升
stretch *v.* 伸展；延伸
catch on 变得流行；理解

Since the late 1980s, three painters who call themselves the Bogside Artists have created large murals in and around the city of Derry, Northern Ireland. Their works are a dramatic ***chronicle*** of the struggle of Northern Ireland's Catholics for civil rights. The murals, which are about 25 feet tall, cover the windowless sides of buildings. One of the most famous, Petrol Bomber, shows a young boy wearing a gas mask. It is a ***scene*** from the 1969 Battle of Bogside, in which British forces clashed with ***protesters***.

从20世纪80年代后期起，三名自称伯格赛德艺术家的画家在北爱尔兰德里市市里及周边创作了大型壁画。他们的作品是对北爱尔兰天主教徒争取公民权利斗争的戏剧性记载。这些壁画大约25英尺高，涂抹在建筑物没有窗户的一侧。最著名的壁画之一，《汽油弹》展示了一个戴着防毒面具的年轻人。它取材于1969年伯格赛德斗争中的一个场景，在那场斗争中英国警察与抗议者之间发生了冲突。

---

chronicle *n.* 编年史；记录
protester *n.* 抗议者；反对者
scene *n.* 场面

9

How to Carry Out a Public Mural Project

Any public mural project must be undertaken by considering its two main aspects—artistic and administrative.

Obtaining ***funding*** is generally the first step in the administrative process. ***Donations***, fund-raising events, and government ***grants*** are typical sources. If the administrators of the project are not

如何实施一项公共壁画项目

承接任何的公共壁画项目必须考虑项目的艺术和管理这两个主要方面。

管理过程的第一步一般是获得资助。捐赠、筹款活动和政府拨款是主要来源。如果工程的管理人员本身并不是艺术家，他们就必须挑选一名艺

funding *n.* 提供资金

donation *n.* 捐款；捐赠物

grant *n.* 拨款；授予物

themselves artists, they must select an artist. This is often done through a competition. Calls for ***entries*** usually state the theme or topic of the mural, which has been decided by the administrators.

Once the artistic team is ***assembled***, members prepare the wall for painting. They clean the surface and repair cracks and holes. Painters then coat the wall with ***primer***, a type of paint that forms a good foundation for painting. The artist measures the wall and prepares a ***maquette***, or scale drawing, that serves as a pattern. Work on the mural can now begin.

In the meantime, the administrators may be promoting the project by holding public relations events, distributing brochures and photos, and sending out press releases on the progress of

---

术家。这常常通过竞聘来实现。在招聘要求中通常会给出已由管理人员决定了的壁画的主题或主旨。

一旦召集了艺术团队，团队成员要把绘画的墙准备好。他们清理墙面，修复裂缝和孔洞。画家接着在墙上刷一层底漆，即一种可以为绘画奠定良好基础的涂料。艺术家测量墙面，准备草图或比例图，充当样板。壁画工作现在可以开始了。

同时，管理人员可通过举办公关活动、发放宣传手册和照片以及发布

---

entry *n.* 参赛作品；条目
assemble *v.* 集合；聚集
primer *n.* 底漆；打底剂
maquette *n.* 初步设计的模型；设计草图

the project. The work does not end with the ***unveiling*** of the mural, however. To ensure that the community can enjoy the mural for years to come, experts recommend that it be cleaned every year to protect it from damage by pollution and weather.

项目进程的新闻稿来推广该项目。然而，这项工作并不以壁画的揭幕而结束。为保证社区居民在未来数年能够欣赏壁画，专家推荐每年都应该清洁壁画以保护其免遭污染和天气的破坏。

unveiling *n.* 除去遮盖物；公开；揭幕式

10

What Happens to Tax Dollars?

Most people are surprised to learn how much money is ***deducted*** from their earnings. Gross pay is a person's total wages or salary, and net pay is what remains after deductions. Where does the deducted money go?

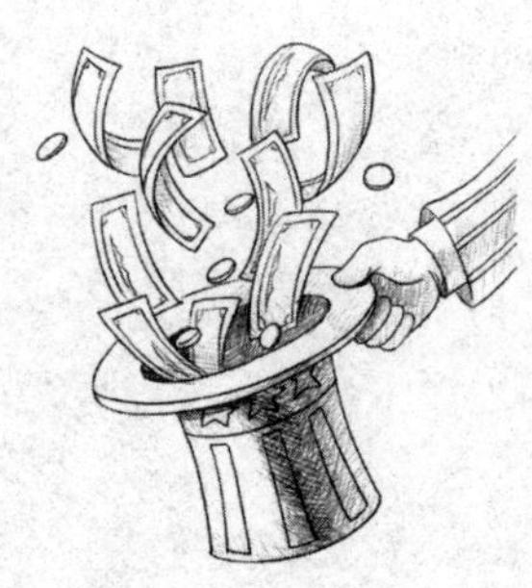

About 6 percent of each ***paycheck*** goes to Social Security, which protects the income

纳税人的钱去了哪儿?

得知自己的收入被扣了多少钱后大多数人很惊讶。工资总额是一个人的全部工资或薪水，而实付工资是扣款以后所剩的。被扣的钱去了哪儿呢?

大约6%的薪水进了社保，用于保障退休人员或残疾人士的收入。缴

deduct *v.* （从总量中）扣除；减去　　**paycheck** *n.* 付薪水的支票；薪水

of retired or disabled people. Workers who pay into the fund receive benefits, usually when they retire. In 2001 nearly one-third of the government's money came from Social Security and Medicare taxes.

Employers also ***withhold*** part of each check for federal income tax. This tax is the federal government's largest source of ***revenue***. In 2001, one-half of the government's money came from taxes paid by individuals.

Taxpayers often wonder what they receive for the money taken from their paychecks. The president must answer that question every year. According to the U.S. Constitution, the president must have ***approval*** from Congress to spend money. The president prepares an annual ***budget*** that summarizes the government's income and suggests how it should be spent. Some expenses, such as

---

纳社保的员工通常在退休时领取退休金。2001年接近三分之一的政府资金来自社保税和医疗税。

雇主也要扣除雇员的部分薪水来缴纳联邦所得税。该税是联邦政府最大的收入来源。2001年，一半的政府资金来自个人所缴纳的税款。

纳税人常常想知道自己薪水被扣了钱而他们为此又得到了什么。总统每年都必须回答这个问题。根据美国宪法，总统必须得到国会的批准才能花钱。总统准备一份年度预算，对政府收入做总结并就如何支配收入提出建议。一些支出是固定的，例如退伍军人津贴和储蓄债券利息。然而，总

---

withhold *v.* 保留；不给

revenue *n.* 财政收入；税收收入

approval *n.* 批准；通过；认可

budget *n.* 预算

veterans' benefits and interest on savings bonds, are fixed. However, the president suggests how much should be spent on ***discretionary*** expenses such as national defense or cancer research.

Circle ***graphs*** are one means the government uses to help people understand the budget. In a circle graph of federal spending, the largest part goes to Social Security; in 2001, for example, nearly one quarter of the budget (23 percent) was returned to taxpayers as Social Security payments. Another large part (19 percent) funded Medicare and ***Medicaid***, the federal health insurance programs for the elderly and the needy. The next largest ***segment*** (16 percent) was spent on national defense. Interest paid on the public debt (13 percent) took almost as big a portion of the budget.

Americans have a right to know how their tax dollars are spent,

---

统可对由其自由支配的费用应有多少提出建议，例如国防或癌症研究方面的费用。

扇形图是政府用来帮助公民了解预算的方法之一。在联邦政府开支的扇形图中，最大的一部分是社会保障。例如在2001年，接近四分之一的预算（23%）作为社会保障金返还给了纳税人。联邦政府开支的另外一大部分（19%）是医疗保险和医疗救助经费，即针对老人和穷人的联邦健康保险计划。联邦政府开支的第二大部分（16%）是国防开支。国债利息支出（13%）占了几乎同样大的比例。

美国人有权知道所缴纳的税款是如何被支出的，因此他们能够获取印

---

discretionary *adj.* 酌情决定的；自由决定的

graph *n.* 图表；曲线图

medicaid *n.* 医疗补助制度

segment *n.* 部分

so copies of the budget are ***available*** in print and online, but these copies contain thousands of pages. Tools such as The Citizen's Guide to the Federal Budget help people find the data they need. Budget Explorer, an online ***tutorial***, allows people to compare their guesses about where their money goes to the actual numbers. Users can also try to balance the federal budget. For more details, they can visit the Web sites of different ***agencies***. These tools are one more means of putting tax dollars to work.

刷好的或在线的预算副本，但这些副本包含上千页。像联邦政府预算公民指南这样的工具可帮助人们找到其所需数据。在线教程“预算探险者”允许人们对缴纳的钱的去处所作的猜测与实际数目进行比较。用户也可试着去平衡联邦预算。关于更多细节，人们可访问不同机构的网站。这些工具是另一种使用税款的方式。

available *adj.* 可得的；有效的

tutorial *n.* 教程；辅导材料

agency *n.* 地区政府；专业行政机构

How to File a Federal Income Tax Return

Each year people who earn money in the United States must file *federal* tax returns. The tax-form package includes *directions* for filing and a worksheet to help people decide whether they must file, but most wage earners who had taxes withheld from a paycheck must file a return.

The Internal Revenue Service (IRS)

如何申报联邦所得税

每年在美国赚钱的人必须申报联邦所得税。整套的纳税申报表包括申报指导以及一个帮助人们决定其是否应当申报的参看表，但大多数薪水中被预扣税款的工薪族必须申报。

国内税务署（IRS）建议纳税人遵循一定的申报步骤。首先，他们必

---

federal *adj.* 联邦的；同盟的　　**direction** *n.* 方向；指导

suggests that taxpayers follow certain steps to file. First, they must collect the necessary information. Interest accrued on savings accounts or other investments is reported on 1099 forms. Taxes withheld by employers are reported on W-2 forms. These forms should arrive in the mail by January 31.

Next, taxpayers must obtain tax forms for filing. Most young taxpayers can file form 1040EZ. The form is available online or at federal offices such as the U.S. Post Office.

Filling out the form should take only a few hours. Line-by-line directions are included, and the IRS provides a ***toll-free*** help line and ***publications*** to answer questions.

After completing the form, the taxpayer should sign and date it.

须收集必要的信息。储蓄账户或其他投资中的利息所得用表1099填报。雇主预扣税款用表W-2填报。这些表应在1月31日之前邮寄至税务署。

其次，纳税人必须获取纳税申报表。大多数年轻的纳税人可填报表1040EZ。这个表可从网上或美国邮政局这样的联邦政府机关获得。

填写表格只需几个小时。表格每一行都有指导，并且国内税务署提供免费帮助热线和出版物来解答疑问。

表格填写完后，纳税人应署名并注明日期。纳税人可邮寄表格或通

---

toll-free *adj.* 不用付电话费的

publication *n.* 出版；出版物

Forms may be mailed in or filed electronically from a home computer. Some taxpayers hire a tax ***preparer***, although this is normally not necessary with the 1040EZ form. Taxpayers who file electronically usually receive their ***refunds*** faster, if refunds are due.

过家庭电脑以电子形式申报。一些纳税人雇用报税员，然而这对申报表1040EZ来说是没必要的。如果退款到期的话，以电子形式申报的纳税人通常更快地收到退款。

---

preparer *n.* 填表人　　**refund** *n.* 退款；偿还

12

The Battle of Britain

Nazi Germany *invaded* Poland in September of 1939. As a result, France and Great Britain *declared* war on Germany, and World War II began. The Nazis, under Adolf Hitler, quickly invaded many European countries. By the summer of 1940, the island nation of Great Britain was the Nazis' only remaining unconquered

不列颠之战

1939年9月，纳粹德国入侵波兰。于是法国和英国对德宣战，第二次世界大战爆发。在阿道夫·希特勒的指挥下，纳粹很快入侵了欧洲许多国家。到1940年夏，英国这一岛国成了纳粹在西欧唯一未能征服的敌人。德国人急于入侵英国。然而，他们计

invade *v.* 侵略；侵入

declare *v.* 宣布；声明

enemy in Western Europe. The Germans were eager to invade Great Britain. However, they planned to destroy the British Royal Air Force (RAF) first so that it could not bomb the German navy as it transported invading forces. The result was the Battle of Britain.

The Luftwaffe—the German air force—began by bombing ports and RAF airfields. Most of the fighting, however, took place in the skies above Great Britain. The Germans hoped to ***lure*** the RAF into the open, where quick German fighter planes would shoot down the planes.

Perhaps Hitler thought that the much smaller RAF could be easily defeated. The Germans had four times as many planes as the British, yet the Battle of Britain ***raged*** for months. During the battle, the Germans lost almost three times as many aircraft as the British.

划先摧毁英国皇家空军，这样德国海军在运送入侵部队时便不会遭到轰炸。结果就是不列颠之战的爆发。

战斗从纳粹德国空军轰炸英国港口和英国皇家空军机场开始。然而，大多数的战斗发生在英国的上空。德国人希望诱使英国皇家空军进入空旷地带，这样德国的快速战斗机可击落英国飞机。

或许希特勒认为规模小得多的英国皇家空军能够被轻易地击败。德国人的飞机比英国人的多四倍，然而不列颠之战持续了数月。在战斗期间，

---

lure *v.* 诱惑；引诱

rage *v.* 猛烈地继续；激烈进行

On some days, the RAF fought as many as five battles. It succeeded in keeping the enemy at bay and saved the country from Nazi ***occupation***.

The RAF, in addition to its ***valiant*** and tireless pilots, used new technology to defend Britain. During World War II, the British introduced an invention that the Germans did not have: radar. It allowed the British to identify approaching planes in all kinds of weather, at any time of day. Thus, RAF pilots could become ***airborne*** before German planes appeared overhead.

Despite the advantages that radar gave Britain, the Luftwaffe inflicted a potentially fatal series of blows when it bombed several

---

德国人损失的飞机要比英国人的几乎多三倍。有时候，英国皇家空军一天要参加五次战斗。它成功地将敌人阻止在海峡对面，使英国免遭纳粹占领。

除了其勇敢的、不知疲倦的飞行员外，英国皇家空军使用了新技术来保卫国家。在二战期间，英国人采用了一项德国人没有的新发明：雷达。它让英国人在各种天气下、在任何时候识别入侵飞机。这样，英国皇家空军飞行员就能在德国飞机飞临头顶上空之前到达空中。

尽管英国有雷达优势，但德国空军的一系列打击可能是致命的，伦敦

---

occupation *n.* 占领

valiant *adj.* 英勇的；勇敢的

airborne *adj.* 空降的；在飞行中的

RAF airfields around London, causing severe damage. In September of 1940, assuming that the bombing had made the RAF ***ineffective***, the German command shifted its attention to bombing London, the capital. Germany hoped that this would force the British to surrender, but the shift in ***tactics*** gave the RAF time to recover. Soon after, it brought down about 60 Luftwaffe planes during a series of large-scale German attacks.

Realizing that it would be unable to ***annihilate*** the RAF quickly, Germany postponed the planned invasion of Great Britain and adopted other tactics aimed at conquering it. Although there was no formal German surrender, the British considered the Battle of Britain a major victory.

周围的几个英国皇家空军机场遭到轰炸并造成了严重破坏。1940年9月，德军统帅部以为轰炸让英国皇家空军失去了作用，便把注意力转向对首都伦敦的轰炸。德国希望这能迫使英国投降，但这一策略转变给了英国皇家空军恢复的时间。很快，它在德国人的一系列大规模攻击中击落了大约60架德国飞机。

意识到不可能很快歼灭英国皇家空军，德国推迟了计划内的对英国的入侵并采取了其他旨在征服英国的策略。尽管德国并未正式投降过，但英国人认为不列颠之战是一场重大胜利。

---

ineffective *adj.* 无效的；不起作用的

tactic *n.* 策略；战略

annihilate *v.* 歼灭；战胜

13

Life During the Blitz

On September 7, 1940, Nazi Germany began heavy, frequent bombing of London and other cities in Great Britain. These attacks, known as the ***Blitz***, finally ended in May of 1941, but during the Blitz the lives of the British people changed ***dramatically***.

At night people followed blackout

大轰炸期间的生活

1940年9月7日，纳粹德国开始猛烈而频繁地轰炸英国伦敦和其他城市。这些攻击被称为大轰炸，最终于1941年5月结束，但在大轰炸期间英国人民的生活发生了巨变。

在晚上人们遵守灯火管制法规，因为灯光会让他们成为德国轰炸机的

blitz *n.* 闪电战；突袭

dramatically *adv.* 突然地；巨大地

regulations because light might have made them targets for German bombers. They pulled black curtains over their windows so that no light could be seen from outside and made special covers for headlights and flashlights to focus narrow beams downward. The British government issued gas masks to everyone, even babies. People carried gas masks with them everywhere.

Many people constructed ***air-raid*** shelters in their backyards; others hid in ***cellars*** or closets during an air attack. London also had hundreds of public air-raid shelters, many in underground subway stations. When an air-raid ***siren*** sounded, people went to the nearest shelter and remained there until they heard the all-clear signal and

---

目标。他们给窗户拉上黑色窗帘以便从外面看不到任何的光，并且为照明灯、电筒制作特别的灯罩以使狭窄的光束向下聚焦。英国政府给每个人都发了防毒面具，甚至是婴儿。人们去哪儿都随身携带着防毒面具。

很多人在自家后院建造防空洞，其他人在空袭时藏在地下室或壁橱里。伦敦还有上百个公共防空洞，许多都位于地下地铁站。当空袭警报拉响时，人们进入最近的掩体并一直待在那里直到听到警报解除信号才能出

---

air-raid *n.* 空袭
cellar *n.* 地窖；地下室
siren *n.* 汽笛；警报器

could come out. Bombs often ***demolished*** entire neighborhoods during an attack.

During the war, many goods, such as butter, were in short supply. The government ***rationed*** those items, and everyone received a specified quantity. People mended clothes or sewed new clothes from old ***fabric***. Despite terror and hardships, the British people found courage to endure the Blitz and the war—and so to ***prevail***.

来。在一次攻击中炸弹常常毁坏整片地区。

在战争期间，很多物品供应紧张，比如黄油。政府对这些物品实行配给制度，每个人得到的量是指定的。人们修补衣服或是用旧布料缝制新衣服。尽管面临恐惧和艰难，英国人找到了承受大轰炸和战争的勇气——取得胜利。

demolish *v.* 彻底摧毁

ration *v.* 配给；定量供应

fabric *n.* 织物；布

prevail *v.* 战胜；获胜

14

Law and Order on the Electronic Frontier

The Internet (Net) is sometimes called the "electronic *frontier*". Like the Old West, this new frontier offers great opportunities and has few rules; but unlike the Old Western towns, the Internet has no *sheriff*. There is no public office with the authority or the power to *tame* it.

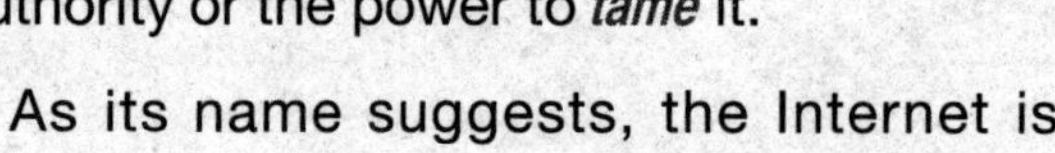

As its name suggests, the Internet is

电子领域的法律和秩序

互联网有时被称作“电子领域”。就像老西部，这个新的领域提供了大量的机会却几乎没有规则可言；但它又不像老西部的那些城镇，在这里没有治安官。互联网里没有拥有职权或能力去驯服它的政府机关。

如它的名字所表明的那样，互联网是计算机网络组成的一个网络。

frontier *n.* 国界；边界；边境

sheriff *n.* 县治安官；城镇治安官

tame *v.* 驯化；驯服；使易于控制

a network of computer networks. It is difficult to ***regulate*** the Net because it has no central control point. The most popular feature of the Internet is the World Wide Web. When people "surf the Web," they connect to an Internet Service Provider (ISP). Each ISP is part of a ***regional*** network that is linked to many larger networks.

At first the Net needed no control. Built in 1969, it was first called the Advanced Research Projects Agency Network (ARPANET). Only scientists working for the Department of Defense used it. The researchers all agreed on two rules: share information and avoid ***commercial*** use. By 1992 ARPANET had grown into the World Wide Web. In 1993 the government asked three private companies to manage the network. Businesses and private citizens could now use the Net.

管理互联网很难，因为它没有中央控制点。互联网最受欢迎的特征是万维网。当人们“浏览网页”时，他们连接到网络服务提供商。每个网络服务提供商是与许多更大的网络连接的局域网的组成部分。

最初，互联网不需要控制。它建于1969年，最初被称作高级研究计划管理局网（阿帕网）。只有为国防部工作的科学家使用它。研究者在两条规则上达成一致：分享信息和避免商业使用。到1992年，阿帕网已经发展成了万维网。1993年，政府要求三家私人公司来管理该网络。企业和普通公民现在可以使用互联网了。

---

regulate *v.* 控制；调节　　**regional** *adj.* 区域的

commercial *adj.* 商业的；营利的

As the Internet grows, lawmakers are not able to keep up. The result is a "policy vacuum". When Manila police arrested the creator of the "Love Bug" ***virus*** in 2000, the Philippines had no laws against computer crimes. The virus stole passwords, so police charged the hacker with credit card ***fraud***.

In 2000 France tried to stop Yahoo from selling Nazi items on the Web. Should France's hate-crime law limit what a foreign company can sell on its Web site? There are many other issues to resolve as well. How does the right to privacy apply to e-mail material written at work? May public libraries block access to sites deemed ***improper*** for children?

As these issues are being argued, who is keeping order on the new frontier? Users follow their own sense of ***ethics*** while ISPs

---

立法者没能跟进互联网的发展。结果是一个“政策真空”。当马尼拉警方于2000年逮捕爱虫病毒创造者时，菲律宾没有针对电脑犯罪的法律。这个病毒盗取密码，于是警方便控告该黑客信用卡诈骗。

2000年，法国试图阻止雅虎在网上出售纳粹物品。法国痛恨犯罪的法律该限制一家外国公司在其网站上所出售的东西吗？还有许多其他问题要解决。隐私权如何适用于工作时所写的电子邮件？公共图书馆可以屏蔽少儿不宜的网站吗？

当这些问题被争论时，谁在这个新的领域维持秩序呢？用户遵循自己

---

virus *n.* 病毒　　**fraud** *n.* 欺骗；诈骗
improper *adj.* 不合法的；不适当的　　**ethic** *n.* 伦理；道德规范

enforce acceptable-use rules. State and national governments pass laws against "cybercrime", scholars propound theories of computer ethics, and computer scientists form groups to promote responsible use of the Net. ICANN, the nonprofit group that manages the Internet, reviews possible reforms.

Despite these valiant efforts, the electronic frontier remains wild. Deceitful people can still ***entrap the unwary***, but taming the Internet poses its own drawbacks by limiting freedom and opportunities on this fast-moving new frontier.

的道德意识，而网络服务提供商执行可接受的使用规则。州政府和中央政府通过针对“网络犯罪”的法律，学者提出计算机道德的理论，而计算机科学家组成小组推动对互联网的负责任使用。互联网名称与数字地址分配这一管理互联网的非盈利机构，研究可能的改革。

尽管有这些无畏的努力，电子领域仍处于疯狂状态。骗子依旧能让不警觉的人落入圈套，但驯服互联网有其自身的弊端，即减少了这个高速运转的领域中的自由和机会。

---

entrap *v.* 使入陷阱　　**the unwary** 粗心的人；不警觉的人

15

Virginia Shea: The "Miss Manners" of the Internet

People who write e-mail messages in ALL CAPITAL LETTERS are often accused of having bad "Netiquette". The term, a ***combination*** of network and ***etiquette***, refers to the standards for polite communication on the Internet. Like the word itself, these standards are based on network technology and common ***courtesy***.

弗吉尼亚·谢伊：互联网的"礼仪小姐"

全用大写字母写电子邮件信息的人常常被人指责为"网络礼仪"不好。这个术语由网络和礼仪这两个词组合而成，指的是在互联网上礼貌交流的标准。就像这个词本身，这些标准建立在网络技术和一般礼节基础之上。

combination *n.* 结合；组合

etiquette *n.* 礼节；礼仪

courtesy *n.* 礼貌；礼仪

When sending e-mail, people see only a computer screen; this makes it easy to ignore the feelings of the person who receives the message. The ***recipient***, too, sees only words on a screen; this means that an angry message can come across more strongly than intended.

Virginia Shea has been called "the 'Miss Manners' of the Internet". Reading columns by Judith Martin, who writes as Miss Manners, shaped Shea's sense of etiquette. Today Shea herself is considered an etiquette expert, and her basic rule is "remember the human". From ***guidelines*** posted by various user groups, she learned that

在发电子邮件时，人们只看到一个电脑屏幕；这容易让人忽略信息接收者的感受。收件人也只看到屏幕上的字；这意味着一条愤怒的信息给人的印象可能要比预期的更加强烈。

弗吉尼亚·谢伊被称作"互联网的'礼仪小姐'"。谢伊的礼节意识受到了其所阅读的朱迪思·马丁专栏的影响，而朱迪思·马丁是以礼仪小姐身份创作。今天谢伊本人被认为是一位礼仪专家，她的基本准则是"记住别人的存在"。她从不同用户组发布的指导方针那里得知全部使用大写

recipient *n.* 接受者；收件人

guideline *n.* 指导方针

using *all caps* is considered "shouting". She suggests that people say nothing in an e-mail message that they would not say in person. Use *emoticons*, such as the "smiley-face" symbol, to show feelings. Use *acronyms*, such as LOL (laughing out loud), to help readers understand when a joke is intended. Shea's book *Netiquette*, written in 1994, is considered the first guidebook to proper Internet manners.

字母被认为是"大喊大叫"。她建议人们当面不会说的话也不要在电子邮件中说。使用表情，例如"笑脸"符号，来表达感情。使用首字母缩写词，例如LOL（大声笑），来帮助读者理解要表达的笑话。谢伊的书《网络礼仪》，写于1994年，被认为是关于网络合宜礼仪的第一本指南。

---

all caps 全部大写

emoticon *n.* 表情符号

acronym *n.* 首字母缩略词

16

Pioneers in Women's Rights

In the United States, the nineteenth century was a period of great social reform. The women's rights movement was among these reforms. Its pioneers were drawn in particular from the ***abolition*** movement. Two of them, sisters Angelina and Sarah Grimké, were ***ardent*** abolitionists. Daughters of slave owners and converts to

女权运动的先驱者

美国的19世纪是一个社会大变革时期。女权运动即是这些大变革之一。它的先驱者多数来自废奴运动。其中的安吉琳娜·葛罗米柯和萨拉·葛罗米柯这对姐妹，是积极的废奴主义者。她们是奴隶主的女儿，同时也是贵格会皈依者，为人直言不讳。1836年当她们公开地讲

abolition *n.* 废除；废止

ardent *adj.* 热烈的；激情的

Quakerism, they were very outspoken. When they spoke in public in 1836 about their own experiences with slavery, they were criticized for stepping beyond the bounds of "proper behavior" for women. This led to their lifelong interest in woman ***suffrage***.

Two other reformers, Lucretia Mott and Elizabeth Cady Stanton, traveled to London in 1840 to attend an international conference on the abolition of slavery. When they arrived, however, they discovered that they would not be allowed to speak and would be forced to sit behind a curtain to watch the ***proceedings***. Such ***blatant*** discrimination sparked in these two women the desire to begin their fight for women's rights.

Along with three other women, Mott and Stanton organized a meeting. It was held in Seneca Falls, New York, in 1848 and was

---

述有关奴隶制的自身经历时，她们因超出了女性"得体举止"的范围而被批评。这导致她们终身对妇女选举权感兴趣。

另外两个改革者，露克瑞蒂雅·莫特和伊丽莎白·卡迪·斯坦顿于1840年到伦敦参加一个废奴运动国际会议。然而，当到了的时候发现她们不能发言并被迫坐在帘子后面观看会议的过程。如此公然的歧视激起了这两位女性开始为女性权力而战的欲望。

连同其他三名女性，莫特和斯坦顿组织了一个会议。这个会议于

---

suffrage *n.* 选举权；投票权　　**proceeding** *n.* 进行；程序

blatant *adj.* 公然的；明目张胆的

attended by 300 people. This meeting became known as the Seneca Falls Convention. Stanton adapted the *Declaration of Independence* to ***proclaim*** that all men and women were created equal. Among the rights that women fought for were the right to property ownership, equal rights in a divorce (including ***custody*** of their children), and (most controversial) the right to vote. From that point on, Mott and Stanton, along with another Quaker reformer, Susan B. Anthony, ***campaigned*** tirelessly for women's rights.

Stanton and Anthony became partners in the fight for women's right to vote. Stanton wrote many of the speeches and pamphlets. Anthony served as organizer and inspirational leader. After the Civil War, when the Fourteenth and Fifteenth ***amendments*** gave African

---

1848年在纽约州的塞尼卡福尔斯举行，有300人参加。这次会议被称作赛尼卡福尔斯会议。斯坦顿改编《独立宣言》中的话宣布男人和女人生来平等。女性为之奋斗的权利包括财产所有权、离婚中的平等权（包括孩子抚养权）和（最受争议的）选举权。从那以后，莫特、斯坦顿连同另外一位贵格会改革者，苏珊·B·安东尼，不知疲倦地开展妇女权利运动。

斯坦顿和安东尼在争取妇女选举权的斗争中成为了伙伴。斯坦顿写了很多演讲和宣传册。安东尼担任组织者和精神领袖。内战后，第十四和第十五修正案给予了黑人公民权利，如选举权，此时斯坦顿和安东尼认为妇

---

proclaim *v.* 宣布；声明
custody *n.* 监护；保管；抚养权
campaign *v.* 参加运动；领导运动
amendment *n.* 修正案

American men the rights of citizenship, such as the right to vote, Stanton and Anthony claimed the same rights for women. Anthony and 150 other women voted in the presidential election of 1872 but were later ***arrested***.

Stanton and Anthony continued their fight. Stanton drafted a woman suffrage amendment in 1878. However, it wasn't until 1920 that the Nineteenth Amendment was ***ratified*** and women won the right to vote. Neither Stanton nor Anthony lived long enough to see their dream become a reality. The right to vote was just the beginning of the struggle for full equality for women.

女应享有同等权利。安东尼和其他150名妇女在1872年的总统选举中参加投票，但随后被捕。

斯坦顿和安东尼继续她们的斗争。1878年，安东尼起草了妇女选举权修正案。然而，直到1920年，第十九修正案才被批准，妇女才赢得选举权。斯坦顿和安东尼两人都未能活着看到自己的梦想成为现实。选举权只是争取妇女完全平等斗争的开始。

---

arrest *v.* 逮捕；阻止

ratify *v.* 批准；认可

17

Educating Safe Drivers

In the first years after the invention of the automobile, driving was fairly ***hazardous***. Cars were not well built, and roads were little more than dirt paths. Through the years, however, a number of factors have improved driving safety. Higher-quality car ***construction***, airbags, and ***restraints*** such as seatbelts and infant seats

教育司机安全驾驶

在汽车发明后的最初几年里，开车是相当危险的。那时汽车制作粗糙，而道路只不过是些土路。然而，随着时间的推移，一系列的因素提高了行车安全指数。高质量的汽车构造、安全气囊和诸如安全带及婴儿车座等安全装置都可拯救生命、减轻损伤。更好的道路和更明亮

hazardous *adj.* 有危险的；冒险的
construction *n.* 构造；结构
restraint *n.* 安全装置

all save lives and reduce ***injuries***. Better roads and brighter lighting help prevent accidents. The safest roads, however, are those that have safe drivers on them.

Safe drivers tend to be experienced drivers. Statistics show that new drivers, especially young drivers, are the most likely to become involved in accidents. Although the laws that govern the licensing of drivers vary from state to state, many states have taken steps to improve driver training.

Among the most advanced approaches are ***intermediate*** or graduated licensing programs. These programs have three parts. The new driver must be at least 15 years old and ***enrolled*** in a driver's education course. New drivers must also pass a written test to obtain a ***permit*** that will allow them to practice driving. Some states

---

的照明可帮助预防事故发生。然而，最安全的公路是那些驾驶者在其上面安全驾驶的道路。

安全驾驶的司机常常是有经验的司机。数据显示驾车新手，特别是年轻驾驶员，最有可能发生事故。虽然州与州之间有关驾驶许可方面的法律不同，但许多州已采取措施加强驾驶员培训。

其中最先进的方法包括过渡的或渐进式考取驾照计划。这些计划包括三部分。考取驾照者必须至少15岁并且参加了驾驶员培训课程。他们还必

---

injury *n.* 伤害；损害
enroll *v.* 注册；参加
intermediate *adj.* 中间的
permit *n.* 许可证；执照

require that a learner's permit be held for a certain number of months before the license test can be administered. All states require a minimum number of hours of practice with an adult licensed driver in the vehicle. Some states require as few as 12 hours of practice; others mandate as many as 100 hours.

In a graduated licensing program, satisfactory ***performance*** on the driving test earns an intermediate license. During the time that new drivers hold an intermediate license, there are severe ***penalties*** for moving ***violations*** such as speeding or failure to stop at stop signs. There may also be restrictions on driving at night, most commonly between the hours of midnight and 5 a.m. At the end of this ***probationary*** period, if the driver has a clean record, he or she

---

须通过笔试以获得允许其练习驾驶的许可证。一些州要求考取驾照者必须在拥有许可证若干个月后才能参加驾照考试。所有州都要求考取驾照者在一名拥有驾照的成人的陪同下进行练车，并对最低时数作了要求。一些州的练车时间要求是至少12小时，其他一些州则强制要求多达100小时的练车时间。

在渐进式考取驾照计划中，驾驶考试中表现良好即获得一个过渡驾照。新手司机在持有过渡驾照期间，如有超速或遇到停车标志时未停车等行车违规将面临严厉处罚。对于夜间开车也可能有限制，最常见的是在午夜及凌晨5点之间的这段时间内。在这个考验期结束后，如果驾驶者无违

---

performance *n.* 表现；业绩
violation *n.* 违反；违背
penalty *n.* 惩罚；处罚
probationary *adj.* 试用的；见习的

receives unrestricted driving ***privileges***.

Such graduated licensing systems are not focused only on teenage drivers. In Maryland, for instance, this approach is called the "rookie driver graduated licensing system". All new drivers, regardless of age, have the same ***obligations*** and are measured by the same standards.

It is important to understand that driver's education is not just for the ***novice*** driver. Even experienced drivers can benefit from a course designed to improve their skills. A number of courses for mature drivers are available through local driving clubs and other organizations.

法记录，他或她即可享有不受限制的驾驶权利。

这种渐进式考取驾照制度不仅仅专注于青少年驾驶者。例如在马里兰州，这个就被称作“新手司机渐进式考取驾照制度”。所有新手司机，无论多大年龄，拥有的职责和接受的衡量标准也一样。

安全驾驶教育不只是针对初学驾驶的人，明白这一点是非常重要的。甚至有经验的司机也能从旨在提高驾驶技能的课程中获益。成手司机可通过当地的驾驶俱乐部和其他机构获得大量此类课程。

---

privilege *n.* 特殊利益；优惠待遇

obligation *n.* 义务；职责；责任

novice *n.* 新手；初学者

18

Cell Phones and Driving

New wireless technologies have cut the cord that bound people to telephones in their homes and workplaces and to telephones in stationary telephone ***booths***. The sounds of telephone signals are everywhere—from ***boulevards*** and department stores to restaurants and theaters. Many of these conversations are

手机和驾驶

新的无线技术让人们使用电话不再局限于家里、工作场所和固定电话亭。到处都是电话的声音——从大街、百货商店到饭店和剧院。许多手机通话会发生在车里。传闻证据表明驾驶时打电话会引起事

booth *n.* 公用电话亭　　**boulevard** *n.* 林荫大道；大街

taking place in cars. ***Anecdotal*** evidence suggests that talking on the phone while driving causes accidents, but it takes more than a few personal tales to establish a link between cell phones and problems on the road.

Scientists, however, are examining this relationship. One study ***demonstrates*** that drivers are more likely to wander from lane to lane and ***collide*** with another vehicle when using car phones. Drivers using phones are also more likely to strike ***pedestrians***. "Hands-free" phones appear to be no safer than hand-held phones. Also, using phones in cars appears to be more dangerous for older people than for younger people.

故，但仅靠一些个人故事是无法把手机与路面交通问题关联在一起的。

然而，科学家正在检验这种关系。一项研究表明开车时使用车载电话的人更有可能来回变换车道、和其他车发生碰撞。开车时打电话的人也更有可能撞到行人。免提电话似乎并不比手持电话安全。另外，与年轻人相比，老年人开车时打电话似乎要更危险。

---

anecdotal *adj.* 逸事的；趣闻的；传闻的
demonstrate *v.* 证明；展示；论证
collide *v.* 碰撞
pedestrian *n.* 行人；步行者

In general, telephones are considered a ***distraction***. Drivers on the phone seem to respond more slowly to changes in traffic or unexpected events. In fact, drivers who talk while they drive are four times as likely to be in an accident as drivers who do not. Drivers using the phone at the time of an accident, moreover, are more likely to suffer a serious or ***fatal*** injury than those who focus only on driving.

总的来说，电话被认为会分散注意力。开车时打电话的人对交通变化或是突发事件所作出的反映似乎要慢很多。事实上，开车时说话的人遇到事故的可能性要比那些不说话的高四倍。此外，驾车时使用电话的人要比那些只专注于驾驶的人在事故中更有可能遭受严重的、致命的伤害。

---

distraction *n.* 注意力分散；心烦意乱　　**fatal** *adj.* 致命的；重大的；毁灭性的

19

Why Did the Ancient Maya Abandon Their Cities?

The ancient Maya built many large cities in the Classic Period, which lasted from about 250 until about 900. Each city had its own king and ruling class. The cities traded with one another but often fought with one another as well. In about 900, the Maya ***abandoned*** many of their cities. ***Archaeologists*** and other scientists

为什么古玛雅人遗弃他们的城市?

在大约从公元250年持续到公元900年左右的古典时期，古玛雅人建造了很多大型城市。每座城市都有自己的国王和统治阶级。城市间相互贸易，但彼此间也经常打仗。大约公元900年，玛雅人遗弃了他们的许多城市。考古学家和其他科学家对于玛雅人离开的原因长期以来

abandon *v.* 抛弃；中途放弃　　**archaeologist** *n.* 考古学家

have long puzzled over why the Maya left. They have formed ***theories*** by examining those cities carefully and studying the settlements that surround them. Researchers think that the populations in some places may have grown so large that people abandoned them because there was not enough food for everyone.

Archaeologists studied ***clues*** from one city and its surroundings to learn what had happened there. In Copán they found many tools dating from 500 to about 1000 and a few tools dating from about 1000 to 1200. They found that no new ***monuments*** had been built after 822. From studying plant remains, scientists concluded that the area around Copán had been farmland. Other evidence suggested that the land was overfarmed. In view of the evidence, the scientists

---

都感到很困惑。通过仔细调查那些城市和研究城市四周的小村落，他们形成了一些理论。研究者认为，在一些地方人口过于膨胀以至于人们因没有足够的食物而遗弃那些城市。

考古学家对一座城市及其周围环境中的线索进行了研究，以了解那里发生了什么。在科藩，他们发现了很多从公元500年至公元1000年左右年间的工具以及一些从公元1000年左右至公元1200年之间的工具。他们发现公元822年以后没有修建新的纪念碑。通过研究植物残骸，科学家们推断科藩周边地区曾是农田。其他证据表明这片土地被垦殖过度。有鉴

---

theory *n.* 理论

clue *n.* （解决问题或疑团时的）线索

monument *n.* 纪念碑；历史遗迹

concluded that a large population lived in Copán until about 1000. As more people farmed the land, the soil lost its richness and produced fewer crops, which caused the Maya who lived there to suffer from ***malnutrition***, as ***analysis*** of skulls shows. As a result, people began to leave Copán in about 1000, but they did not completely abandon the city until about 1200.

War also may have caused the Maya to abandon some of their cities. For example, it is thought that a ***rival*** city, Caracol, may have once conquered Tikal. Then, after more than 100 years had passed, Tikal returned to power, and the ruling family built temples to honor its victory. However, by the end of the 800s, Tikal was no longer powerful. Its inhabitants left the city. Some archaeologists and

---

于此，科学家们得出结论直到公元1000年左右在科藩居住着大量人口。随着更多的人耕种土地，土壤不再肥沃、产量减少，这导致住在那儿的玛雅人营养不良，而对他们头盖骨的分析表明了这一点。结果，在公元1000年左右人们开始离开科藩，但直到公元1200年他们才完全遗弃这座城市。

战争同样导致玛雅人遗弃他们的许多城市。例如，据称蒂卡尔可能曾被竞争对手卡拉科征服过。然后过了100多年，蒂卡尔再度掌权，其统治家族建造了神殿来纪念胜利。然而，到9世纪末，蒂卡尔不再强大。住在

---

malnutrition *n.* 营养失调；营养不良

analysis *n.* 分析；分解；验定

rival *adj.* 竞争的

historians think that war may have broken out again and caused the citizens to leave.

Although we do not know for certain why many ancient Maya abandoned their cities, we may find some clues by ***observing*** today's Maya. Modern Maya still live in the lands, including Mexico and Guatemala, that their ancestors ***occupied***. Many present-day Maya practice a variety of ancient beliefs and customs, such as farming practices. Studying their beliefs and practices may help scientists discover more about ancient Mayan culture.

那里的人离开了。一些考古学家和历史学家认为战争可能再次爆发并导致了居民的离开。

虽然我们不确定为什么许多古玛雅人遗弃他们的城市，但我们可以通过观察今日的玛雅找到一些线索。现代玛雅人仍然生活在他们祖先居住过的土地上，这片土地包括墨西哥和危地马拉。许多今日的玛雅人实践着各种古老的信仰和习俗，比如说耕作方式。研究他们的信仰和习俗可帮助科学家对古玛雅文化有更多的发现。

---

observe *v.* 观察 **occupy** *v.* 居住

20

Remnants of the Past

Today one can visit several ancient Mayan city-states (or at least the *excavated* portions of them). One such city, Tikal, has about 3,000 buildings—such as temples, pyramids, palaces, and houses—many of them still buried. Archaeologists have restored parts of Tikal, including several *plazas* and buildings linked by broad

过去留下的遗迹

今天人们可以参观多个古玛雅人城邦（或者至少是这些城邦被挖掘出的部分）。蒂卡尔就是一个这样的城市，它有大约三千幢建筑——例如神殿、金字塔、宫殿和房屋——其中很多仍被埋在地下。考古学家修复了蒂卡尔部分城区，包括几个由宽阔马路连接的广场和建筑物。王宫位于城市中心。离其较远处的是北阿科罗普利斯，那里有八座神

excavate *v.* 挖掘；发掘

plaza *n.* （城市中的）露天广场

roads. Royal palaces stand at the center of the city. Beyond them is the North Acropolis, which includes eight temples. Between the palaces and the North Acropolis is a ball court.

In Chichén Itzá, one can also see a ball court, but the Mayan courts look only vaguely similar to today's basketball courts. The court in Chichén Itzá ***resembles*** a capital I. Several stone rings, each with a narrow opening in its center, jut out from the stone walls of the ball courts, high above the ground.

Like Tikal, Chichén Itzá has temples, but one can also see several buildings there, including the Caracol ***Observatory***, that the Maya built to watch the skies. After walking up many stairs and going into the round observatory, one walks up a ***spiral*** staircase into a small room. The room has windows through which one can watch the Sun, Moon, planets, and stars, about which the Maya kept detailed records.

殿。在王宫和北阿科罗普利斯之间是一个球场。

在奇琴伊察人们同样能看到一个球场，但玛雅人的球场与今天的篮球场仅仅是大体上相似。奇琴伊察的那个球场像大写字母 I 。几个高于地面的石环从球场的石墙突出来，每个石环在其中央有一狭窄的开口。

像蒂卡尔一样，奇琴伊察也有神殿，但人们在那里还能看见几幢建筑，其中包括一个玛雅人建造用来观察天空的卡拉科尔天文台。在爬了很多台阶进入圆形天文台后，人们通过一个螺旋状阶梯来到一个小房间。房间里有窗户供人观测太阳、月亮、行星和恒星，玛雅人对观测做了详细记录。

---

resemble *v.* 像

observatory *n.* 天文台；气象台；瞭望台

spiral *adj.* 螺旋形的；盘旋的

21

Harvest Festivals from Many Cultures

Throughout history, people who have *relied* on agriculture as their way of life have held harvest festivals to celebrate a good growing season. Although fewer people are involved in farming today, the tradition of harvest celebrations continues. People from different *backgrounds* have adapted practices from other lands.

不同文化中的丰收节

在整个历史发展过程中，依靠农业为生的人们都会举办丰收节来庆祝好收成。尽管现在从事农业的人变少了，但这个庆祝丰收的传统仍然继续。来自不同背景的人适应了其他国家的做法。

rely *v.* 依赖；依靠　　background *n.* 背景

In some cultures, the harvest festival takes place during the full moon closest to the fall ***equinox***. One such occasion is Têt-Trung-Thu (pronounced tet-troong-thoo), which is the ***Vietnamese*** Mid-Autumn Festival. The event has become a special holiday for children. Young people receive gifts and candy while they enjoy ***parades*** and other forms of entertainment. The Vietnamese continue the tradition of making star lanterns and animal masks.

Another autumn harvest festival is Sukkoth (pronounced so-o-kôt´ in Hebrew). (Sukkoth comes from sukka, meaning “temporary shelter”.) The celebration takes place in September or October, the time of harvest in Israel. It ***commemorates*** when the Hebrews wandered in the wilderness, living in huts that could easily be

---

在一些文化中，人们经常在距秋分最近的那个月圆之夜庆祝丰收节。“T ê t-Trung-Thu”即越南的中秋节(读作tet-troong-thoo)就是这样的一个时间。这个活动已经成为了孩子们的特别节日。年轻人在欣赏着游行和其他娱乐形式时，会收到礼物和糖果。越南人为庆祝这一节日制作星形灯笼和动物面具的传统仍然存在。

另一个秋天的丰收节是犹太结茅节（在希伯来语种读作so-o-kôt'）。（Sukkoth来源于sukka，意思是“临时的避难所”。）以色列人在9月或10月，也就是他们收割的时候庆祝这个节日。这个节日是用来纪念西伯来

---

equinox *n.* 春分；秋分

parade *n.* 游行

Vietnamese *adj.* 越南的；越南人的

commemorate *v.* 庆祝；纪念

moved. Today Jews often build small huts with roofs made of branches. During the eight-day celebration, they may eat, pray, and even sleep in these sukkoth.

Many North American peoples gave thanks for the harvest during the Green Corn festival. The Cherokee usually held their festival in July. Before the celebration, women performed a religious dance. The people built an ***arch*** of green branches to cover the grounds, and everyone drank a ***purifying*** drink. This festival lasted up to four days. Another famous Native American festival is the Iroquois Strawberry ***Ceremony***, a time of thanksgiving for the strawberry harvest, which usually takes place in May.

The people of Europe also celebrated harvest festivals. In Poland,

---

人住在容易移动的小屋中、在荒野中游荡的日子。现在，犹太人仍然时常建造房顶由树枝制成的小屋。在为期八天的庆祝活动中，他们可能在这些临时的避难所里吃东西、祈祷，甚至睡觉。

很多北美人在绿玉米节期间感恩丰收。彻罗基族人经常在7月举行庆丰收活动。在庆祝活动之前，女人们表演宗教舞蹈。人们搭建一个绿树枝拱门覆盖在地面上，每个人都要喝一杯净化的饮料。这个节日持续多达4天。另一个著名的印第安节日是易洛魁人的草莓仪式，它是感恩草莓丰收的节日，经常在5月举行。

欧洲人也庆祝丰收节。例如，在波兰，人们经常在收获快结束的时

---

arch *n.* 弓形；拱形；拱门

purify *v.* 净化；精制

ceremony *n.* 典礼；仪式

for example, Dozynski, or Harvest Day, took place about August 15, at the end of the harvest. A village girl wore a crown made of straw. The mayor of the town then put a rooster on top of her crown. As the girl led a ***procession*** away from the fields, people listened closely: If the rooster ***crowed***, they believed they would have good luck in the coming year. In another Polish harvest tradition, a female farm worker gave the local noble a wreath made of grain. After he received the gift, the celebration began. Festivals are still held today to honor these ***traditions***.

候，一般在8月15日庆祝“Dozynski”，或者丰收节。一个乡村女孩带上稻草制成的王冠。镇长把一只大公鸡放在女孩的王冠上面。当女孩带着队伍离开田地的时候，人们都会仔细倾听：如果公鸡打鸣了，他们就相信下一年一定会有非常好的运气。在另一个波兰人的丰收传统中，农场女工要给当地的贵族一个由谷物制成的花冠。在贵族收到礼物后庆典便开始了。今天，人们仍然庆祝这些节日来表达对传统的敬重。

---

procession *n.* 队伍；行列

crow *v.* 啼叫；报晓

tradition *n.* 惯例；传统

22

Morocco: Past and Present

Morocco's long history includes periods of peace, wealth, and strong government as well as times of ***violence***, ***bankruptcy***, and weak leadership. Although Berbers have lived in this northwestern part of Africa for more than 3,000 years, many other peoples have settled there too. The Roman Empire once

摩洛哥：过去和现在

摩洛哥的悠久历史中既包含了和平、富有和政府强大时期，也包含了充满暴力、破产和领导不力时期。尽管柏柏尔人在这个非洲西北部生活了3 000多年，也还有许多其他人在那里定居。罗马帝国曾经拥有过部分摩洛哥的领土。其他人跟随罗马人去了那里，但大部分人只

violence *n.* 暴力行为；暴乱

bankruptcy *n.* 破产

included parts of Morocco. Other peoples followed the Romans, most staying only a short time. ***In contrast***, the Arabs swept into Morocco in about 680, bringing with them Islam—today the state religion of Morocco. About 100 years later, an Arab ruler united Berbers and Arabs to form the first Moroccan state.

The union did not last, however, and for hundreds of years, a succession of Arab and Berber ***dynasties*** ruled in Morocco. Some dynasties ruled empires that stretched across northern Africa and reached into Spain and Portugal. Then, in 1415, Portugal captured one of Morocco's ports. Thereafter Portugal and Spain gained increasing control over ***coastal*** Morocco, while the Moroccans battled to drive the Europeans from the country. By the 1800s, France also

---

住了很短的一段时间就离开了。与此相反，阿拉伯人在680年左右席卷了摩洛哥，并带来了伊斯兰教——现在伊斯兰教成为了摩洛哥的国教。大约100年以后，一个阿拉伯统治者联合柏柏尔人和阿拉伯人在摩洛哥建立了第一个国家。

然而，联合并没有持续多久，几百年间，阿拉伯和柏柏尔王朝交替统治着摩洛哥。一些王朝统治下的帝国领土一度横跨非洲北部直达西班牙和葡萄牙。后来，在1415年，葡萄牙侵占了摩洛哥的一个港口。尽管摩洛

---

in contrast 相比之下

dynasty *n.* 王朝；朝代

coastal *adj.* 沿海的；海岸的

had become interested in Morocco.

As a result of ***treaties***, military victories, and a bankrupt Moroccan government, France and Spain had gained control over Morocco by the early 1900s. France, and to a lesser ***extent*** Spain, kept control for many years. During that time, the French built roads, railroads, and new towns. They reformed the legal system and modernized the government. Settlers from France and Spain governed the country. Moroccans were left with no voice in the government. Dissatisfied and angry, they demanded independence, ***staging*** revolts and rioting against foreign control.

Finally, in 1956, Morocco gained its independence. When Hassan II became its king, he adopted the first Moroccan ***constitution***. Hassan II worked to solve many of Morocco's problems, including

---

哥人努力想把欧洲人赶出他们的国家，但葡萄牙和西班牙却对摩洛哥沿海地区取得越来越多的控制。到19世纪，法国也对摩洛哥产生了兴趣。

一系列的条约、军事上的胜利和摩洛哥政府的破产使得法国和西班牙在20世纪早期攫取了摩洛哥的控制权。法国和西班牙控制了摩洛哥很多年，尽管后者的控制程度要比前者小。在那段期间，法国人在摩洛哥修建了公路、铁路和新的城镇。他们改革法律体系并使政府现代化。来自法国和西班牙的殖民者统治了这个国家。摩洛哥人在政府中毫无发言权。他们既不满又愤怒，他们要求独立，进行造反和发动暴动反对外国统治。

最终，在1956年摩洛哥获得了独立。当哈桑二世成为了摩洛哥的国

---

treaty *n.* 条约；协议；谈判

extent *n.* 范围；程度

stage *v.* 举行；筹划

constitution *n.* 宪法；体制；章程

unemployment and high inflation. He passed laws to increase Moroccan ownership and employment in companies doing business in Morocco. In rural areas, he ***redistributed*** foreign-owned farms to Moroccan farmers. He also ***revised*** a code of laws to give women more rights. Hassan II did not solve all of Morocco's problems during his lifetime, but many experts agree that he left the country in better condition than it had been in when he came to power. Today his son, Mohammed VI, is furthering his goals. Mohammed VI has also made education for all Moroccan children a priority, in part because he considers education the basis for progress.

王时，他通过了摩洛哥的第一部宪法。哈桑二世致力于解决摩洛哥的很多问题，包括失业和通货膨胀。他通过法律增加摩洛哥人在摩洛哥境内公司里的所有权和就业。在农村，哈桑把外国人的农场重新分配给了摩洛哥农民。他还重新修订了法典，给予女人更多的权利。哈桑没有在他的有生之年解决掉摩洛哥的所有问题，但是很多专家认为，哈桑当政后国家情况比他刚刚掌权时有很大的好转。现在，他的儿子穆罕默德六世正在进一步实现他父亲的目标。穆罕默德六世还优先考虑了摩洛哥所有孩子的教育问题，这是因为在某种程度上他认为教育是发展的基础。

---

redistribute *v.* 重新分配；再区分

revise *v.* 修订；修正

23

The Journeys of Ibn Battuta

Born in Morocco, Ibn Battuta was a traveler and writer who lived from 1304 to about 1370. At that time, travel was difficult and often unsafe. Disease, ***shipwrecks***, and attacks by ***robbers*** were common ***perils***. Ibn Battuta traveled about 75,000 miles during his lifetime. He visited the lands of every Muslim ruler and a

伊本·巴图塔游记

伊本·巴图塔是一个摩洛哥旅行家兼作家，他生于1304年，卒于1370年前后。在伊本·巴图塔生活的那个时代，旅行很困难，而且常常很危险。疾病、海难和强盗的攻击都是非常常见的危险。伊本·巴图塔一生的旅行路程大约有75 000英里。他去过每一个穆斯林统治

shipwreck *n.* 船只失事；海难

robber *n.* 强盗；盗贼

peril *n.* 危险；冒险

few other places as well, journeying to places that today are 44 countries.

Ibn Battuta's travels began when he made his first ***pilgrimage*** to Mecca. According to Islam, all Muslims who can make a trip to Mecca must do so. In 1325, Ibn Battuta decided to make his. During the trip, which lasted about a year and a half, he studied with teachers and judges.

After his pilgrimage, he continued to travel, visiting places in Africa, Asia, and Europe. Finally he went to India, where he became a judge. After several years in India, Ibn Battuta ***resumed*** his visits to

---

的地域，还去了其他一些地方，他旅行过的地方遍及了现在的44个国家。

伊本·巴图塔的旅行始于他第一次去麦加朝圣。按照伊斯兰教的教规，所有能够去麦加的穆斯林都必须去朝圣。在1325年，伊本·巴图塔决定去朝圣。在这次持续了大约一年半的旅程中，他与教师和法官共同学习。

朝圣之后，伊本·巴图塔继续旅行，他去了非洲、亚洲和欧洲的许多地方。最后他到了印度，在那里他成为了法官。在印度停留几年后，

---

pilgrimage *n.* 朝圣之行；朝拜

resume *v.* 重新开始；继续

other countries, including China. In the late 1340s, he returned to Morocco after more than 20 years.

After two more ***expeditions***, Ibn Battuta returned to Morocco ***permanently***. He told his stories to its ruler, the sultan. At the sultan's request, he ***dictated*** his adventures to a famous literary figure who ***refined*** Ibn Battuta's simple prose style. Today the book provides a detailed account of life in the 1300s.

伊本·巴图塔开始重新拜访其他国家，其中也包括中国。14世纪40年代末，在离开20多年后，他回到了摩洛哥。

在又进行了两次探险后，伊本·巴图塔永远地回到了摩洛哥。他把自己的故事讲给了统治者苏丹。在苏丹的请求下，伊本·巴图塔把他的冒险经历口述给了一位有名的文学人物，并由他对伊本·巴图塔简单的文风进行了完善。今天，这本书为人们提供了14世纪人们生活的详细记载。

expedition *n.* 有组织的旅行
permanently *adv.* 永久地；长期不变地
dictate *v.* 口述；听写
refine *v.* 使提练；完善

24

"Reading" Textiles to Reveal the Past

Technicians on the popular television show CSI: Crime Scene *Investigation* solve murders by analyzing every scrap of evidence. They may examine a thread found on a victim's body under a microscope. Learning the source of the fiber may help them find the killer. Archaeologists also analyze fibers, remains,

通过"读懂"纺织品来揭示过去

在流行的电视节目"犯罪现场调查"中，技术人员通过分析每一个证据破获谋杀案。他们可以通过显微镜检查受害人身上被找到的丝线。研究这些纤维的来源可以帮助他们找到凶手。考古学家也分析

technician *n.* 技术员；技师

investigation *n.* 调查；调查研究

and other evidence, but the ***mysteries*** that they try to solve are thousands of years old.

One such mystery was why fibers from ***mummified alpacas*** found at El Yaral, Peru, are so much softer than those from modern animals. Under a projection microscope, the fibers measured 17.9 micrometers, almost as fine as ***cashmere***, yet fibers from modern alpacas and llamas are so coarse that they are used only in blankets. The discovery of the 1,000-year-old mummies at El Yaral sparked a program to restore the purebred lines created by the Incas. Because cashmere sells for $70 a pound, restoring the fine-fiber breeds could boost Peru's economy.

Even scraps of cloth can reveal how people of ancient cultures

---

纤维、遗骸和其他的证据，但是他们要解答的却是有几千年历史的奥秘。

其中一个这样的奥秘是为什么在秘鲁的厄尔·亚拉尔发现的木乃伊化的羊驼身上的纤维比现代动物身上的纤维更加柔软。在投影显微镜下测量出的纤维长度是17.9千分尺，这个尺寸的纤维可以和羊绒媲美。然而，现代羊驼和美洲驼身上的纤维却十分粗糙，只能用来织地毯。在厄尔·亚拉尔发现的千年木乃伊引发了一个恢复生产印加人创造的纯种羊驼的计划。因为羊绒的出售价格是70美金1磅，恢复纤维优质的羊驼品种可以推动秘鲁经济发展。

甚至是布的碎片也可揭示古代文化中的人是怎样生活和工作的。艾

---

mystery *n.* 迷；神秘

alpaca *n.* 羊驼

mummify *v.* 将……做成木乃伊

cashmere *n.* 羊绒；开士米

lived and worked. Irene Good, a textile archaeologist, has developed new ways of working with ancient textiles. She reads ancient ***garments*** by counting threads and re-creating the methods used to produce them. The weavers of ancient Peru were so skilled that one piece of fabric might reveal several techniques. Their work was prized, so it was passed down from generation to generation. Good has almost 5,000 complete pieces to study.

Darrell Gudrum reads ancient textiles by interpreting their designs. One ***mantle***, or cloak, from ancient Peru had more than 120 symbols on it. The cloak showed many ***constellations***, so Gudrum compared them with those on the Inca calendar. He concluded that the cloak was a "farmer's almanac", showing when to plant and harvest crops.

琳·古德，一个纺织物考古学家，开发了一种研究古代纺织物的新方法。她通过对线的数量进行计算和再现过去制造它们的方法来解读古代衣服。古秘鲁的织工技巧很熟练，一件织物便可展示几种技术。他们的工作很受重视，被一代代地传承下来。古德收集了差不多5 000件完整的织物进行研究。

达雷尔·古德隆通过了解织物的图案来解读古代纺织物。一件古秘鲁的斗篷或披风上面有120多个符号。其中包括许多星座。于是古德隆把它们与印加日历上的那些星座相比较。他得出的结论是这个披风是一本"农民的历书"，告诉人们什么时候耕种、收获庄稼。披风上还有一些符号与

---

garment *n.* 衣服

mantle *n.* 斗篷；披风

constellation *n.* 星座；星群

The mantle also had symbols related to religious rituals.

Another way to learn about the past is to study living weavers. Women in Peru still use techniques passed down through oral tradition. Nilda Callañaupa founded the Center for Traditional Textiles of Cusco to ***preserve*** this heritage. She has already found a village where weavers use a rare technique thought to be ***extinct***. The center documents the methods and symbols used by weavers in ***remote*** villages such as Pitumarca. It also creates opportunities for young women to learn these traditions. The textile collection will help people in Peru and around the world learn to read the past from pieces of cloth.

宗教仪式相关。

另一个了解过去的方法是研究活着的织工。在秘鲁，妇女仍然使用通过口述传统传承下来的技术。尼尔达·科拉劳帕成立了库斯科传统纺织物中心，保护这项遗产。她已找到了一个村庄，那里的织工使用一项被认为失传了的罕见技术。她的中心记录了生活在像皮图马卡这样偏远村庄里的织工所使用的方法和符号。这也为年轻妇女学习这些传统创造了机会。这些纺织物收集品将帮助秘鲁以及世界各地的人们通过一块块布来了解过去。

---

preserve *v.* 保护；保存
extinct *adj.* 绝种的；灭绝的
remote *adj.* 遥远的；偏僻的

25

Elizabeth Barber, Textile Archaeologist

Pots and spear points can survive for centuries. Fabric is so *fragile* that, in the past, archaeologists sometimes did not even try to preserve it. Now experts such as Elizabeth Wayland Barber are showing that textiles can *reveal* information about the past.

Barber is a leader in the new field of textile archaeology. One of her special

伊莉莎白·芭柏，纺织物考古学家

罐子和矛尖可以存留几个世纪。织物却非常易碎，以致过去考古学家有时甚至都不试图去保存织物。但是现在的专家们，例如伊莉莎白·韦兰·芭柏，指出纺织物可以揭示过去的信息。

芭柏是纺织物考古学这一新领域的领导者。她对史前的纺织物和衣物特别感兴趣。在13年中，她主要研究比她自己的拇指指甲还小的古老的纺织物。1991年出版的《史前纺织物》和1994年出版的《女人们的工作》

fragile *adj.* 脆的；易碎的

reveal *v.* 透露；显示

interests is ***prehistoric*** cloth and clothing. For 13 years, she worked mostly with pieces of old cloth smaller than her thumbnail. Her interests are reflected in the titles of two early works: *Prehistoric Textiles*, published in 1991, and *Women's Work*, published in 1994.

In 1995 Barber was one of three Western scholars invited to view the Cherchen mummies. These mummies, found in a desert area of China, are at least 3,000 years old. The hot, dry desert preserved their skin and the clothing that had been buried with them.

One pattern in the fabrics found with the mummies was much like Celtic tartans. Could these Caucasian-looking mummies have migrated to China from Europe? Barber confirmed that the fibers and weaving techniques in the fabrics originated in Europe. She also used ***linguistic*** clues to trace the ***nomads'*** journey to Asia. Her book on the subject, *The Mummies of Ürümchi*, was published in 1999.

是她的两部早期作品，这两本书的标题反映了她的兴趣爱好。

1995年，芭柏成为了被邀请至车尔臣考察木乃伊的三名西方学者之一。这些木乃伊是在中国的沙漠地带被发现的，至少有3 000年的历史。干燥、炎热的沙漠保护着这些木乃伊的皮肤以及和他们一起埋葬的衣物。

在木乃伊身上发现的织物中有一种图案非常像现在的凯尔特格子呢。这些白人模样的木乃伊可能是从欧洲迁居到中国的吗？芭柏证实了这些织物的纤维和纺织技术的确源于欧洲。她还使用了语言线索去追溯游牧民去往亚洲的行程。关于这一问题她撰写了《乌鲁木齐的木乃伊》一书，该书于1999年出版。

---

prehistoric *adj.* 史前的；陈旧的

linguistic *adj.* 语言的；语言学的

nomad *n.* 游牧民；流浪者

26

Careers in the Museum Industry

A person seeking a new career opportunity might consider looking in a museum. Museums provide jobs in fields such as research, management, ***graphic*** arts, public relations, education, preserving, ***cataloging***, fund-raising, and construction. A museum may have one employee or thousands.

博物馆行业中的工作

正在寻找工作机会的人可以考虑去博物馆看看。博物馆在研究、管理、图像艺术、公共关系、教育、保护展品、编辑目录、筹款和建筑等领域都可提供工作岗位。一所博物馆里可能有一名或者上千名工作人员。

graphic *adj.* 绘图的；图画的

catalog *v.* 编目录；登记

Many museum workers do not work directly with the objects in the museum; for example, the staff of a finance department prepares budgets and financial reports. Accountant and bookkeeper are typical positions. Staffers in the development department, meanwhile, work to increase museum membership and donations and to plan fund-raisers, such as dances or ***auctions***. Publications department ***personnel*** may write newsletters, ***brochures***, or books.

Some museums have an education department responsible for planning talks, teaching workshops, directing tours, or training tour guides.

People who prefer to work directly with a museum's collection have many career options. A person who pays attention to detail may enjoy being a ***registrar***, the person who keeps track of the

---

许多博物馆的工作人员并不直接与馆中的物品接触。例如，财务部的工作人员负责准备预算和财务报告。会计和记账员就是典型的这样的岗位。同时，发展部的员工负责增加博物馆的会员数和捐款，并筹划筹款活动，比如举办舞会或拍卖会。出版部的工作人员可能负责撰写业务通讯、宣传手册或书籍。

一些博物馆还有教育部门，负责安排演讲、开办研讨会、指导参观或培训导游。

喜欢直接和博物馆内的收藏品接触的人有许多工作可选。注重细节的

---

auction *n.* 拍卖

brochure *n.* 小册子

personnel *n.* 人员

registrar *n.* 登记员；记录员

objects in a museum. Registrars keep records of objects, noting what they are, when and how they were obtained, and whether they are on loan to another museum or on display.

Curators are the people responsible for a museum's collection. One of their duties is to choose items for exhibits; then they work closely with designers who plan the best way to arrange exhibits. Other specialists do things such as arrange lighting or build display cases. Expert ***craftspeople*** can also find jobs re-creating historic buildings, such as the Pilgrim village at Plimoth Plantation.

A museum also often employs ***conservators*** to repair and take care of its collection. Many conservators are specialists who care for one

---

人可能会喜欢成为登记员，负责了解博物馆中物品的动态。登记员要对物品作记录，标注出物品是什么、什么时间和怎样得到的，是否被其他博物馆借去或者正在展出。

馆长是对博物馆中收藏品负责的人。他们的职责之一是为展览挑选展品；然后他们和负责设计以最佳方式安排展品的设计者们一起紧密工作。其他专家做安排照明或者制作展示柜这一类的工作。熟练的手工艺人也能找到重建像普利茅斯庄园的清教徒村这样的建筑工作。

博物馆也经常雇用管理员去修复和照看馆中收藏品。许多管理员是照

---

curator *n.* 馆长；管理者

craftspeople *n.* 手艺人；工匠

conservator *n.* 保护者；管理员

kind of item, such as books or paintings. The Henry Ford Museum employs many conservators, including some who are experts in caring for ***antique*** cars.

Some historic homes, such as George Washington's home in Mount Vernon, have gardens, farms, and woods, as well as buildings. Gardeners are employed to care for the grounds and ***livestock*** handlers to care for farm animals.

Museums offer many other career opportunities too. They may have gift shops where sales assistants sell books, postcards, and other items or restaurants where meals are prepared and served. Depending on one's interests, a museum could be a great place to look for a job.

看某种展品的专家，如书籍或绘画作品。亨利·福特博物馆雇用了很多管理员，其中包括许多照看古董车方面的专家。

许多有历史性意义的住宅，例如乔治·华盛顿的芒特·弗农庄园，有花园、农场和树林，当然，还有建筑物。这些地方雇用许多园丁和家畜训练员分别来照看土地和农场中的动物。

博物馆里也有许多其他的工作机会。它们会有礼品店，需要卖书、明信片和其他物品的售货员，或者餐厅里准备食物和招待客人的服务员，根据个人的兴趣，博物馆是个找工作的好地方。

---

antique *adj.* 古式的；古董的；古老的

livestock *n.* 牧畜；家畜

27

Becoming a Museum Volunteer

Yvonne loved visiting museums and looking at the ***exhibits***. She wanted to work in a museum after she ***graduated*** from college, so she ***consulted*** museum Web sites on the Internet to find out about the kinds of skills she would need. She soon learned that by volunteering at a museum she could gain experience and learn how a

成为一名博物馆志愿者

伊冯喜欢去博物馆观赏展品。她希望自己大学毕业后能在博物馆工作，因此，她查阅了因特网上的博物馆网站，想了解有关在博物馆工作所需要的各种技能。她很快知道了在博物馆做志愿者可以获得

exhibit *n.* 展览品；陈列品

graduate *v.* 毕业；获得学位

consult *v.* 查阅；咨询

museum operates.

Yvonne searched the Web for a nearby museum and was pleased to see that the museum had many volunteer opportunities. She read that she could water plants in the greenhouses or answer phones in an office. She could volunteer at the information desk, greeting visitors and giving them directions. She could volunteer in the public relations department, ***assembling*** press packets. Then she saw a volunteer position that fit her interests perfectly. She could work as a ***docent***, giving tours to visitors and telling them about the museum's collection.

Without ***hesitation*** Yvonne called the museum and asked how to

---

很多经验，同时还能了解到博物馆如何运作。

伊冯在网上搜索到了附近的一座博物馆，她非常高兴地看到这座博物馆有许多志愿者名额。她了解到自己可以在温室里给植物浇水，或者在办公室接听电话。她还可以在服务台当志愿者，接待来访者并为他们指引方向。同时，她也可以在公关部做志愿者，准备成套宣传材料。然后，她看到了一个完全符合她兴趣的志愿者岗位。她可以当一名讲解员，指导参观者进行观光，为他们讲解博物馆中的收藏品。

伊冯没有犹豫就给博物馆打了电话，并询问了如何成为一名讲解员。

---

assemble *v.* 汇集；收集

docent *n.* 讲师；讲解员

hesitation *n.* 犹豫

become a docent. She learned that she would first have to complete an ***application*** and arrange for an interview. If accepted as a docent, she would then take classes for eight months to learn about the museum's collection. After that she would be ready to give her first tour. ***Flushed*** with excitement, Yvonne requested an application. Already she could picture herself giving her first tour.

她被告知应该先填写申请表，然后会有一个面试。如果申请被接受，她将接受为期8个月的课程，学习博物馆中的收藏品。课程结束后她就可以准备首次带游客参观博物馆了。由于兴奋伊冯脸都红了，她要了一张申请表。她已经在想像自己第一次带参观者游览博物馆的情形了。

application *n.* 应用；申请

flush *v.* 脸红

28

The Russian Revolution of 1917

In order to understand why the Russian *Revolution* of 1917 occurred, one must first understand what life was like in the Russian Empire in pre Revolutionary days. For hundreds of years, ***czars***, or ***emperors***, ruled Russia. The czar and other wealthy landowners represented only 20 percent of the population. Most of the people were

俄国1917年革命

要了解俄国1917年革命为什么会发生，必须首先了解革命前夕俄罗斯帝国人民的生活状况。几百年来，沙皇或皇帝统治着俄国。沙皇和其他富有的土地所有者只代表全国20%的人口。而大多数人民

revolution *n.* 革命
emperor *n.* 皇帝；君主
czar *n.* 沙皇

poor peasants and workers, who lived in crowded conditions and could neither read nor write. These people had ***virtually*** no say in their government. The czar's rule was ***absolute***, and his advisors wanted no changes in the system. Although an elected ***parliament*** (Duma) existed, most of its members were wealthy landowners. The czar could dismiss it anytime he wanted and then demand the election of a new one. Over the years, the people became ***resentful*** of the czar's nearly complete control over their country and their lives. Many longed for improved working conditions or more land. Others wished for changes in the structure of the government.

World War I added to the hardships. By 1917 Russia had been

都是贫穷的农民和工人，他们生活在拥挤的环境下，既不会阅读，也不会书写。事实上这些贫苦的人在政府中完全没有发言权。沙皇的统治是绝对的，他的幕僚希望这种体制不会改变。尽管有一个通过选举产生的议会（杜马）存在，但大多数杜马成员都是富有的土地所有者。沙皇可以随时解散议会，然后要求选举新的杜马。多年来，沙皇对国家和人民近乎完全的控制使人们非常愤慨。许多人渴望改善工作环境或者获得更多的土地。另外一些人希望改变政府结构。

一战使俄国人民的生活更加困苦。到1917年俄国已经经历了三年的

---

virtually *adv.* 事实上；实际上

absolute *adj.* 绝对的；完全的；专制的

parliament *n.* 议会；国会

resentful *adj.* 怨恨的

at war for nearly three years. People were suffering from shortages of food and fuel, among other supplies. Many educated people believed that the czar's decisions, such as appointing weak government officials and leaving the capital to command the armed forces, had ***doomed*** the war effort.

In March 1917, shortages of bread and coal caused the Russian people to revolt. Instead of subduing the ***rioters***, Russian soldiers joined them. With the czar away fighting, parliament appointed a temporary government. A committee of soldiers and workers soon assumed control.

The czar surrendered to the revolutionaries. In the ***ensuing*** months, they organized their forces, setting up a number of councils called ***soviets***. Members were workers, peasants, soldiers, and

---

战争。除了其他生活用品之外，人们也忍受着粮食和燃料的短缺。许多受过教育的人认为沙皇的一系列决定已经注定了战争的失败结局，这些决定包括任命软弱的政府官员、离开首都指挥武装部队等。

在1917年3月，面包和煤炭的短缺导致了俄国人的反抗。士兵没有镇压暴乱者，反而加入其中。由于沙皇正在远方参战，议会任命了一个临时政府。一个由士兵和工人组成的委员会很快夺取了国家的控制权。

沙皇向革命者投降。在接下来的几个月里，革命者组织了武装力量，建立了许多被称作苏维埃的理事会。理事会是由工人、农民、士兵和来自

---

doom *v.* 注定；使失败

ensuing *adj.* 随后发生的；随后的

rioter *n.* 暴徒；暴民；骚乱者

soviet *n.* 苏维埃（代表会议）；委员会

others. Vladimir Ilich Lenin, a revolutionary leader who believed in ***communism***, urged the soviets to seize the power of the temporary government. He promised peace, land for the peasants, and factories controlled by the workers. World War I, strikes, and other crises ***plagued*** the temporary government.

Finally, Lenin thought that the time was right to seize power. Early in November, the well-organized revolutionaries stormed the temporary government's ***headquarters***, arrested its members, and took control of Russia. Although Lenin and his followers seized power quickly, they then had to fight a civil war and control peasant uprisings and workers' strikes in order to hold onto and build their power.

其他阶层的人组成的。革命领袖弗拉基米尔・伊里奇・列宁信仰共产主义，呼吁苏维埃夺取临时政府的政权。他许诺给予人民和平，还土地于农民，让工人掌管工厂。第一次世界大战、罢工和其他危机使临时政府遭到了重创。

最终，列宁认为夺取政权的时机到了。11月初，精心组织的革命者猛攻临时政府的总部，逮捕了临时政府的成员，控制了俄国。尽管列宁和他的追随者很快获得了政权，但他们又要应对内战、农民起义、工人罢工来巩固政权。

---

communism *n.* 共产主义　　**plague** *v.* 困扰；折磨

headquarter *n.* 总部

29

The Theory of Communism

The word communism comes from a Latin word meaning "common" or "belonging to all". Many people have supported communist ideals such as equality of work and shared *profit*. In the 1800s, Karl Marx and Friedrich Engels turned the *concept* of communism into a theory of revolution.

共产主义理论

共产主义这个词来自于一个意义为“公有”或“共同所有”的拉丁词汇。很多人都拥护如工作平等和共享利润这样的共产主义理想。在19世纪卡尔·马克思和弗里德里希·恩格斯把共产主义这一概念变成了一个革命理论。

profit *n.* 利益；利润

concept *n.* 观念；概念

Marx and Engels were aware of the poor pay, long hours, and dangerous working conditions of European factory workers. Both men believed that the workers' situation would not change without a ***struggle***. The men ***reasoned*** that a minority of people owned or controlled the means of production, such as land, factories, and money. Most people were workers who controlled nothing except their ability to work. The ***ruling*** class kept most of the profits from the goods produced. Marx and Engels argued that the ruling class would not give up its power and profits freely. Therefore, they said, workers must take them. Marx and Engels thought that, with workers controlling the government, society change so that all people would

---

马克思和恩格斯知道欧洲工人收入很低，工作时间很长，工作环境危险。两人都认为不经过斗争，工人的境遇是不会改变的。他们得出推论，认为少数人拥有或控制土地、工厂和金钱等生产资料。占人口大多数的工人除了劳动力外一无所有。统治阶级从工人生产的商品中获得大部分利润。马克思和恩格斯认为统治阶级不会主动地放弃自己的权力和利益。因此，他们指出工人们必须自己夺取它们。他们认为，如果工人控制了政

---

struggle *n.* 斗争；努力
reason *v.* 推断；推理
ruling *adj.* 统治的；管理的；支配的

live in peace and be equal and ***prosperous***.

Vladimir Ilich Lenin believed in communism, but he thought that the workers needed a group of ***dedicated*** revolutionaries to lead them. In 1917 in Russia, Lenin put his theory of communism into practice. He led into revolt people who believed in a classless society in which all would live well.

府，社会就会改变，这样所有人都将生活安宁、平等富裕。

弗拉基米尔·伊里奇·列宁信仰共产主义，但是他认为工人需要一群有奉献精神的革命者来领导他们。1917年，在俄国，列宁把他的共产主义理论付诸于实践。他领导那些相信在无产阶级社会都能过上好日子的人们进行了起义。

---

prosperous *adj.* 富裕的；成功的　　**dedicated** *adj.* 献身的；一心一意的

30

Hands-off Policies of Calvin Coolidge

Calvin Coolidge was president of the United States from 1923 to 1929. His policies made him popular with the public and big business, two groups that wanted less government control of their affairs. During his ***presidency***, Coolidge ***approved*** plans to cut government spending and reduce federal taxes, including those

卡尔文·柯立芝的不干预政策

卡尔文·柯立芝是1923年至1929年的美国总统。他的政策受到公众和大企业的欢迎，这两个群体都希望政府少控制他们的事务。在其担任总统期间，柯立芝批准了削减政府开支和降低联邦政府税收

presidency *n.* 总统职位任期

approve *v.* 批准；赞成

for business. His secretary of the treasury, Andrew W. Mellon, thought that big business would profit more if it paid less in taxes. He believed that the profit would help the nation as a whole. At first, the tax cuts did encourage business to increase the production of goods, such as cars and radios. However, businesses eventually produced more goods than people could afford to buy.

While in office, Coolidge ***vetoed*** many bills that would have ***regulated*** business. Like many Americans of his time, he believed that state and local governments should regulate business and that the federal government should step in only when absolutely necessary.

Coolidge did, however, think that the federal government should promote business interests at home and abroad, and he approved federal spending when it would build a base for business. He

---

的计划，包括为企业减税。他的财政部长安德鲁・W・梅隆认为如果纳税减少大企业将受益更多。他相信企业所得到的好处会对整个国家有帮助。起初，减税的确鼓励了企业增加诸如汽车、收音机等商品的生产。然而，企业最终生产了的商品要比人们能买得起的多很多。

在任期间，柯立芝否决了很多约束企业的法案。他与那个时代的很多美国人一样，认为州和地方政府应该约束企业，而联邦政府只应该在绝对必要时才介入。

然而柯立芝的确认为联邦政府应该在国内外维护企业利益。他批准可

---

veto *v.* 否决；禁止　　　　**regulate** *v.* 控制（尤指通过规则）

supported ***tariffs***, or taxes, on foreign-made goods to protect American manufacturing. As a result, Americans bought American-made goods because they were cheaper than goods made in foreign countries.

Although he was willing to develop a sound base for business, Coolidge opposed government efforts to help business directly. During the 1920s, the price of farm goods fell because of a ***surplus*** of crops. Many farmers went into debt and lost their land. Coolidge, however, vetoed farm-aid bills that would have allowed the government to buy surplus crops. He also opposed a bill to aid flood ***victims***. Private business interests such as ***contractors***, he thought, would get most of the aid.

为企业奠定基础的联邦政府开支。他支持对外国制造的商品征收关税或税收，来保护美国制造业。结果，美国人购买美国制造的商品，因为它们比在外国制造的商品便宜些。

尽管他愿意为企业建立稳定的基础，柯立芝反对政府直接帮助企业的做法。在20世纪20年代，农产品的价格由于农作物过剩而下跌。许多农民负债，失去了土地。然而，柯立芝否决了允许政府购买多余农作物的农业救助法案。他也反对救助洪水受害者的法案。他认为像承包商这样的私人企业将得到大部分救助。

---

tariff *n.* （政府对进口货物征收的）关税

surplus *n.* 过剩；盈余

victim *n.* 受害人；牺牲者

contractor *n.* 承包人；承包商

Believing that business would take care of itself, Coolidge set up the ***Division*** of Trade Practice Conference within the Federal Trade Commission. The division organized business conferences at which members of a particular industry reached agreements about what defined fair-trade practices within their industry. The agreements effectively ***blocked*** individuals and companies from bringing lawsuits claiming that companies were engaging in unfair trade practices.

Although American spending had increased by the time Coolidge left office, economic prosperity was to ***crumble*** before the end of the 1920s.

柯立芝相信企业会管好自己，他在联邦贸易委员会中成立了贸易协商部门。这个部门组织协商会议，使各行业的成员在其本行业中就公平贸易达成协议。这些协议有效地阻止了个人和公司提起的一些企业正参与不公平贸易这一类的诉讼。

虽然到柯立芝离任时美国人的开支增加了，但经济繁荣在20世纪20年代末之前即将崩溃。

---

division *n.* 部门 **block** *v.* 阻挡；阻止
crumble *v.* 崩溃；崩塌

31

The Stock Market Crash of 1929

As the 1920s progressed, American businesses were ***thriving*** and the economy booming. Many people were investing money in the stock market and buying shares of stock.

Between 1925 and 1929, the value of most stocks more than doubled. ***Investors*** who sold their shares when the price increased made a great deal of money.

1929年股市崩盘

随着20世纪20年代的时间推移，美国企业生意兴隆，经济欣欣向荣。许多人把钱投入股市，购买股份。

在1925年至1929年期间，大多数股票的价格翻了一倍多。那些在价格上涨时卖掉股份的投资者赚了一大笔钱。这导致许多投机者借钱投资股

thriving *adj.* 兴盛的；繁荣的

investor *n.* 投资者

This led numerous ***speculators*** to borrow money to invest in the stock market. They planned to sell their shares when the stock increased in value. However, this ***injection*** of money into the market ***inflated*** stock prices beyond the worth of the stocks. On October 24, 1929, the surge in stock prices turned into a plunge. By October 29, stock prices had decreased even further, causing numerous investors to panic and sell their stocks, even though the stocks were worth less than their purchase price.

By the end of the year, investors had lost billions in the stock market crash. Banks and businesses that had lost heavily in the stock market closed. Millions of people lost their savings when banks failed. As banks and businesses closed, the people they employed lost their jobs. The stock market crash of 1929 contributed to the decline of the American economy and the resulting Great Depression, which would last into the 1940s in the United States.

市。他们计划在股票价格上涨时卖掉股份。然而，这笔注入股市的钱让股票价格超出了股票的价值。1929年10月24日，股票价格的猛涨变成了暴跌。到10月29日，股票价格更进一步下跌，造成无数投资者恐慌并卖掉他们的股票，即使股票价格比所购价格低很多。

到这一年末，投资者在股票崩盘中损失了几十亿美元。在股市损失严重的银行和企业纷纷倒闭。上百万人因银行倒闭而失去储蓄。由于银行和企业倒闭，它们的雇员也失去了工作。1929年的股市崩盘是美国经济衰落的部分原因，由此产生的大萧条在美国持续到20世纪40年代。

---

speculator *n.* 投机者；投机商　　**injection** *n.* （资金或资源的）注入

inflate *v.* 抬高（物价）；涨高；夸大

32

The Santa Fe Trail and the Opening of the Southwest

In the early years of the nineteenth century, the United States extended only as far west as the ***border*** between Kansas and Missouri. At that time, most of what is now Texas, New Mexico, Arizona, and southern California was part of Mexico. Mexico was ruled by Spain, a country that was ***hostile*** to trade between

圣菲贸易通道和西南部的开放

在19世纪纪初，美国向西只延伸至堪萨斯州和密苏里州交界处。那时，现在的德克萨斯州、新墨西哥州、亚利桑那州以及南加利福尼亚的大部分地方属于墨西哥。墨西哥由西班牙统治，而西班牙对它统治下的墨西哥省份与美国之间的贸易持敌对态度。结果，美国与西南部的

border *n.* 边界　　**hostile** *adj.* 敌对的；怀敌意的

its Mexican provinces and the United States. As a result, travel between the United States and the Southwest was limited. Mexico's independence from Spain in 1821 opened up opportunities for daring and ***innovative*** traders and for ***eventual*** U.S. settlement of the Southwest.

In contrast to Spanish policy, the Mexican government was open to trade with the United States. Aware of the money to be made, William Becknell, a Missouri trader, transported a load of goods from western Missouri to Santa Fe, New Mexico, in 1821. His route followed an old trail long used by Native Americans, fur ***trappers***, and explorers. It meandered westward along the Arkansas River and then turned southward through the mountains. At Santa Fe, Becknell

---

往来被限制。1821年墨西哥从西班牙取得独立，这为胆大的、创新的贸易者提供了机会，也为美国最终取得西南部提供了机会。

与西班牙的政策比起来，墨西哥政府愿意与美国进行贸易。意识到有钱可赚，密苏里州商人威廉·贝克纳尔于1821年把大量的货物从密苏里西部运到了新墨西哥的圣达菲。他走的是印第安人、毛皮猎人以及探险家长期使用的一条古老路线。它沿着阿肯色河向西曲折前进，然后向南转穿过群山。在圣达菲，贝克纳尔发现人们长时间得不到日常用品和工业品。

---

innovative *adj.* 富有创新精神的；采用新观念的　　**eventual** *adj.* 最后的；最终的

trapper *n.* 捕杀动物者（尤指为获取毛皮）

found a population long deprived of supplies and manufactured goods. His ***merchandise*** fetched high prices.

Becknell planned a second trip. This time, instead of pack horses, he used mule-drawn wagons. He also decided to follow a shorter route, which turned south some 150 miles east of La Junta, Colorado. This route, however, crossed an ***expanse*** of desert. Becknell and his party nearly died of thirst before they found the Cimarron River. This new route ***sliced*** 10 days from the trip. Soon 75 percent of the traffic between Missouri and Santa Fe used this route. Becknell's route became known as the Santa Fe Trail. His pioneering journeys opened Santa Fe for trade and earned him the nickname Father of the Santa Fe Trail.

他的商品卖了高价。

贝克纳尔计划再去一次。这次他用骡拉货车代替驮马。他还决定走一条更短的线路。这条线路在科罗拉多州拉洪塔以东150英里处向南拐。然而，这条线路要穿越一大片沙漠。贝克纳尔和他的同伴在发现西马伦河之前差点渴死。这条新线路让行程减少了10天。不久，密苏里州和圣达菲之间75%的交通使用这条线路。贝克纳尔开辟的这条线路被称作圣菲贸易通道。他的拓荒之旅为圣达菲打开了贸易之门，并为他赢得了“圣菲贸易通道之父”的绰号。

---

merchandise *n.* 商品；货物

expanse *n.* 一大片（海洋、天空、土地等）

slice *v.* 大幅度削减；大量降低

Word of the eager buyers in Santa Fe spread quickly. Within a few years, the Santa Fe Trail became a ***bustling*** trade route. Traffic increased during the Mexican-American War (1846–1848), when the trail became an important supply route. After the American victory, the Southwest became U.S. ***territory***. Army ***forts*** along the trail ensured a steady demand for military supplies, and business continued to boom. The arrival of the transcontinental railroad in Santa Fe in 1880 proved to be the beginning of large-scale settlement of the Southwest. Trains replaced the Santa Fe Trail, as people and goods began to travel by rail.

圣达菲人极想购买东西这消息很快传开了。不到几年，圣菲贸易通道成了一条繁忙的贸易线路。在墨美战争（1846—1848）期间，这条通道成了一条重要的补给线路，交通量增加。美国胜利后，西南部成了美国的领土。通道沿线的军队要塞确保了对军需用品的稳定需求，商业继续繁荣。1880年，横贯大陆的铁路修至圣达菲，在西南部大规模定居开始了。人员和货物开始通过铁路运输时，火车取代了圣菲贸易通道。

---

bustle *v.* 奔忙；繁忙

territory *n.* 领土；领域

fort *n.* 堡垒；碉堡

33

Tejanos

Like all Southwestern states, Texas culture has a distinctly Mexican flavor. Despite their cultural influence, Tejanos, as Texans of Mexican ***descent*** are known, have suffered ***discrimination*** at the hands of the state's Anglo, or non-Hispanic, residents.

This was not always the case. While

特哈诺人

与所有西南部州一样，德克萨斯州文化有着独特的墨西哥风味。尽管特哈诺人作为墨西哥人的后裔对德克萨斯州文化有影响，但他们受到美国白人或非西班牙裔居民的歧视。

情况不总是这样的。当德克萨斯还是墨西哥的一部分时，特哈诺人

descent *n.* 血统；祖先　　**discrimination** *n.* 歧视；差别对待

Texas was part of Mexico, Tejanos were independent ***ranchers***. However, as Texas increased its ties with the United States—becoming a state in 1845—large numbers of settlers of European descent traveled there. Tejanos became a minority in their own state. They were pushed to the ***outskirts*** of financial and cultural life, and many had their lands unfairly seized. Since the 1800s, many Tejanos have occupied the lower rungs of the economic ladder. They have worked in hard jobs in farming, construction, ranching, and the service industry. Many have endured ***segregation*** and have been denied voting rights.

But Tejanos have retained their culture, much of which grew out of their ranching past. Their artisans make fine saddles, saddle

---

是自食其力的牧场主。然而，随着德克萨斯与美国的联系增加，在1845年成为美国的一个州，大批欧洲移居者去了那儿。特哈诺人在自己的州成了少数民族。他们被推到经济和文化生活的边缘地带，很多人的土地被不公平地掠夺了。从19世纪起，许多特哈诺人在经济阶梯中地位较低。他们在农业、建筑业、牧业以及服务业中从事艰苦工作。许多人忍受着种族隔离，没有选举权。

但特哈诺人保留了他们的文化。其大部分文化产生于过去经营牧场的经历。他们的工匠制作上好的马鞍、鞍褥以及马刺。他们的康芬特音乐

---

rancher *n.* 牧场主 **outskirt** *n.* 外围；边缘（远离中心的部分）
segregation *n.* 隔离；分离

blankets, and ***spurs***. Their conjunto music, with its accordions and polka-like rhythms, is popular. ***Ceramics***, woven goods, quilts, and yard ***altars*** are familiar Tejano folk arts. Perhaps the best known of their folk art objects are the lightweight, brightly adorned hollow sculptures called piñatas. At parties blindfolded children try to break open a piñata with a stick to reach the candy inside.

使用手风琴，节奏如波尔卡舞曲般，很受欢迎。陶瓷、编织品、被褥和庭院祭坛是为人熟知的特哈诺民间艺术品。最有名的民间艺术品叫做彩饰陶罐，它质量轻、装饰鲜艳，而且中空。在宴会上，被蒙上眼睛的孩子会试着用棍子砸开彩饰陶罐去拿里面的糖果。

spur *n.* 马刺；靴刺

altar *n.* 祭坛；神坛

ceramic *n.* 陶瓷；陶瓷制品

34

Let the Play Begin!

Legend has it that the performing arts began when a Greek singer named Thespis invented ***tragedy***. In 534 b.c., Thespis was performing a ***hymn*** to the god Dionysius. Such hymns, called ***dithyrambs***, were usually sung by a lead singer and a chorus. Thespis added a speaking actor. Performances at the annual Dionysian

让表演开始！

传说表演艺术是从一位名叫泰斯庇斯的希腊歌唱家创造悲剧时开始的。公元前534年，泰斯庇斯为酒神狄奥尼索斯唱赞美诗。被称作酒神赞歌的赞美诗通常由一个主唱和一个合唱队来歌唱。泰斯庇斯增加了一个解说演员。一年一度的酒神节上的表演很快包括了有三名演员

tragedy *n.* 悲剧

hymn *n.* 赞美诗；圣歌

dithyramb *n.* （古希腊酒神节唱的）赞美酒神的颂歌

festival soon included plays with three actors as well as the standard hymns. By 449 b.c., the Greeks were giving prizes to the best actor and the best playwright at the festival. A modern word for actor—thespian—recognizes the debt today's ***drama*** owes to Thespis.

Performing in a Greek play required ***stamina***. Because each play had only three actors, performers had to play several roles. Chorus members both sang and danced. Being in the chorus for the many performances given at a festival was said to be as demanding as competing in the Olympic Games.

The Theater of Dionysius in Athens could hold 20,000 people. Even those in the front rows were quite a distance from the

---

参加的戏剧演出以及标准的赞美诗。到公元前449年，希腊人在节日庆典上给最佳演员和最佳剧作家颁奖。现代演员的单词——thespian——承认了当今戏剧源自于泰斯庇斯。

在希腊戏剧中演出要求耐力。因为每部戏剧只有三名演员，表演者不得不扮演几个角色。合唱队成员既唱歌又跳舞。据说要想加入到为节日里的众多表演担当合唱的合唱队，其要求就像参加奥林匹克运动会比赛一样高。

雅典的狄奥尼索斯剧院能容纳20 000名观众。就是坐前排的观众离演

---

drama *n.* 戏剧；剧本　　**stamina** *n.* 耐力；耐性；持久力

actors. Performers used grand gestures and wore masks so that they could be seen by everyone in their huge audience. Tragic actors wore ***dignified*** robes and masks that allowed clear speech. Comic actors wore short costumes that let them move freely and masks designed to make them look ugly or silly. Sometimes the chorus was ***costumed*** to look like animals. Although most actors no longer wear masks, dramas are still classified as tragedies or comedies, and special-effects makeup is still popular. Another tradition that survives from ancient Athens is political ***satire***. Actors sometimes wore masks that made them look like well-known public figures. One was worn by the playwright Aristophanes. Aristophanes had a feud with the dictator Cleon and he wrote

---

员也有一段距离。表演者动作幅度大，戴着面具，这样庞大的观众群中的每一个人都能看到他们。悲剧演员穿着庄严的长袍，戴着能让人清楚说话的面具。喜剧演员则穿可让其自由移动的短戏服，戴着旨在让他们看起来丑陋或愚蠢的面具。有时合唱队穿成动物的样子。尽管大部分演员不再戴面具，戏剧仍被分为悲剧或喜剧，有特别效果的打扮依旧受欢迎。从古雅典存留下来的另一个传统是政治讽刺作品。演员有时戴上面具，让其看起来像知名人士。剧作家阿里斯多芬尼斯就会这么做。他与独裁者克里昂不和，写了几部攻击克里昂的戏剧。据称，演员们都非常害怕克里昂而不敢

---

dignified *adj.* 庄重的；庄严的

costume *v.* 给……穿上服装

satire *n.* 讽刺；讽刺文学

several plays attacking Cleon. Supposedly, the actors were all too afraid of Cleon to appear in Aristophanes' play *The Knights*, so the playwright played the role of the ruler himself.

Another legacy of the ancient Greeks is the deus ex machina, or "god of the machine". If a playwright was having trouble with the plot, he might have a god appear through a trap door. The god would ***rescue*** the main character and resolve any tricky plot situations. Modern writers might not call on ***divinities***, but they do sometimes use unlikely ways to end a story. A character or an event that brings a complicated plot to an improbable conclusion is still called a deus ex machina.

出演阿里斯多芬尼斯的戏剧《骑士》，剧作家本人不得不自己出演统治者这个角色。

古希腊人的另一项遗产是在戏剧情节中牵强扯入用于解围的人或事件，或"解围之神"。如果剧作家在情节方面遇到麻烦，他可以让神通过暗门出现。神会拯救主要角色，解决任何棘手的情节问题。现代作家可能不会呼唤神灵，但有时他们的确是用不太可能的方式结束一个故事。以不可能的方式结束复杂情节的一个角色或者一个事件仍旧被称作"deus ex machina"。

rescue *v.* 营救；援救

divinity *n.* 神；神力

35

The Fearless Comedy of Aristophanes

Everything known today about the early Greek ***comedies*** comes from the plays of one man, Aristophanes. The works of other comic writers from the fifth century b.c. have been lost, but 11 of Aristophanes' plays ***survive***. His comedies often won first prize at the Dionysian festival, and they are still performed today.

阿里斯多芬尼斯的无畏的喜剧

今天所知的希腊早期喜剧的一切都来自于一个人，他就是阿里斯多芬尼斯。公元前5世纪的其他喜剧作家的作品都失传了，但阿里斯多芬尼斯有11部喜剧流传了下来。他的喜剧经常在酒神节上获得第一名，甚至今日还在上演。

comedy *n.* 喜剧

survive *v.* 幸存；继续存在

The Acharnians is the earliest of his surviving comedies. Written during one of the many wars between Sparta and Athens, it has a main character who decides to make peace with the enemy. This play is considered the first antiwar comedy.

In *The Clouds*, the playwright takes on the famous ***philosopher*** Socrates. An old man ***enrolls*** in "Socrates' Thinking Shop" to learn to argue. He decides that his son would get more out of the lessons. The son then beats his father and uses Socratic arguments to ***justify*** his disrespect.

In *The Wasps*, Aristophanes attacks a favorite target—the legal system. An old man spends so much time watching trials that his

---

《阿卡奈人》是他存留下来的最早的作品。这部作品写于斯巴达与雅典战争期间，其中有一个决定和敌人讲和的主要角色。这个戏剧被认为是第一部反战喜剧。

在《云》中，作者提及了著名的哲学家苏格拉底。一位老人报名了“苏格拉底的思想所”去学习辩解。他认定他的儿子将从课程中获得很多。儿子随后打了父亲，并用苏格拉底的辩术来证明自己的不敬是对的。

在《马蜂》中，阿里斯多芬尼斯攻击了一个最喜欢的目标——法律体制。一位老人在观看审判上花了太多时间以至于他的儿子最终强迫他待在

---

philosopher *n.* 哲学家；哲人

enroll *v.* 注册；参加

justify *v.* 证明……是正当的

son finally forces him to stay home. The old man is ***desperate*** to escape until his fellow jurors appear as a swarm of wasps to rescue him.

Aristophanes also invented satire. *The Knights* ***portrays*** the ruler of Athens, Cleon, as a dishonest dictator. Cleon took the playwright to court, but Aristophanes continued to ***satirize*** him in other plays.

家里。这位老人不顾一切地想逃走，直到他的陪审员同伴们像一群马峰一样出现来拯救他。

阿里斯多芬尼斯还发明了讽刺。喜剧《骑士》把雅典统治者克里昂描绘成了一个欺诈的独裁者。克里昂把作者告上了法庭，但阿里斯多芬尼斯依旧在其他戏剧中讽刺他。

---

desperate *adj.* 不顾一切的；极度渴望的

portray *v.* 扮演；描绘

satirize *v.* 讽刺；挖苦

36

Bicycle Use Around the World

In countries around the world, people ride bicycles. For some people, bicycles are ***recreational***, but others use them as transportation. Bicycles are one of the most energy-efficient and cost-effective means of transportation. They need no fuel, are much less expensive than cars, and are easy to ***maneuver*** through crowded places.

自行车在世界范围内的使用

在世界各国，人们骑自行车。对一些人来说，自行车是用来娱乐休闲的，而其他人则把它们用作交通工具。自行车是最节能、最划算的交通工具之一。它们不需要燃料，比汽车便宜很多，易于在拥挤的地方操控。

recreational *adj.* 娱乐的；消遣的

maneuver *v.* 移动；操控

More than 2,000 police departments in the United States have bicycle ***patrols***, as do police departments in many other countries. One fully ***equipped*** police bike costs about $1,200. Compare that price to about $25,000 for a patrol car. Bicycle patrols are useful for policing areas such as parks and for ***zipping*** through crowded city streets.

Although only a small percentage of Americans use bicycles for transportation, bicycles are a major mode of transportation for people in other parts of the world, such as Asia. In many Asian cities, people use bicycles and foot-operated vehicles such as ***rickshaws*** and cyclos to transport paying customers or hundreds of pounds of freight. In some Chinese cities, bicycle trips account for more than half of all trips. Local governments in Japan built millions of bicycle

---

在美国，超过2 000个警察局进行自行车巡逻，就像许多其他国家的警察局那样。一辆装备齐全的自行车大概要花1 200美元。把这个价格跟巡逻警车的价格比较下吧，一辆巡逻警车需要25 000美元。自行车巡逻对巡视公园这样的区域以及在拥挤的城市街道上穿梭有帮助。

虽然只有很小比例的美国人使用自行车作为交通工具，自行车在世界的其他地方，比如亚洲，是人们的主要的交通方式。在许多亚洲城市，人们使用自行车以及黄包车、三轮车这样的脚踏车辆来运送付钱的客人或是上百镑重的货物。在中国的一些城市，骑自行车旅行占了所有旅行的一半

---

patrol *n.* 巡逻；巡查
equip *v.* 装备；配备
zip *v.* 迅速地行动（或移动）
rickshaw *n.* 人力车；黄包车

parking spaces at train stations to encourage people to use bicycles instead of cars to reach the train station.

The bicycle is also widely used in Europe. The Netherlands is probably the country in which the bike is most widely used. There are many reasons for this. First, in the Netherlands, as in the rest of Europe, ***gasoline*** is very expensive. Second, most of the land is flat, which makes riding a bike there much easier than in countries with mountains and hills. Third, houses are often very close to businesses. This makes it easier for people to use bicycles to get to and from work. Perhaps most important, the Dutch government has built thousands of miles of bicycle paths and bike ***lanes***. As a result, factory workers, farmers, shop owners, accountants, lawyers, and teachers ride bicycles to work.

以上。在日本，当地政府在火车站建了上百万的自行车停车位来鼓励人们骑自行车而不是开车去火车站。

在欧洲，自行车同样被广泛使用。荷兰大概是自行车使用最广泛的国家，这其中有许多原因。首先，在荷兰，像欧洲其他地方一样，汽油非常贵。其次，大部分地域平坦，这使得在荷兰骑自行车要比在山地、丘陵国家容易得多。第三，住房离企业很近。人们骑自行车上下班很容易。或许最重要的是，荷兰政府建造了上千英里长的自行车专用道和脚踏车道。因此，工厂工人、农民、店主、会计、律师和教师都骑自行车上班。

---

gasoline *n.* 汽油

lane *n.* 车道；航线

In Africa people also often use bicycles. In some parts of Africa, programs have encouraged the use of bicycles as taxis to transport shoppers to markets, children to school, and sick people to medical ***facilities***. A driver can transform a bicycle taxi into an ambulance by attaching a ***trailer*** to it.

Other means of transportation may come and go, but the bicycle, invented in the early nineteenth century, has clearly stood the test of time.

在非洲，人们也经常使用自行车。在非洲一些地方，有计划鼓励把自行车当出租车来使，用自行车送购物者去商店，送学生上学，送病人去医疗机构。骑车人加个拖车就能把自行车变成救护车。

其他交通工具可能有兴有衰，但发明于19世纪初的自行车很明显经受住了时间的考验。

---

facility *n.* （供特定用途的）场所

trailer *n.* 拖车；挂车

37

Military Uses of the Bicycle in World War II

World War II required massive movements of armies and supplies. ***Stealth*** was ***essential*** sometimes so that the enemy would not hear approaching troops, and sometimes moves were into places that were ***inaccessible*** by trucks and tanks. Cars, trucks, and tanks run on fuel, but often there was none. The bicycle

二战中自行车在军事上的使用

第二次世界大战要求军队和补给的大规模移动。秘密行动有时很有必要，这样敌人听不到军队接近，并且有时得去卡车和坦克难以到达的地方。汽车、卡车和坦克靠燃料来驱动，但经常没有燃料。自

stealth *n.* 秘密行动；秘密

essential *adj.* 至关重要的；必需的

inaccessible *adj.* 难达到的；难接近的

solved these and other problems. It required no fuel, and it was quiet and easy to maneuver. Cyclists did not need regular roads, and they could go many places where trucks and tanks could not. Perhaps most important, a soldier could easily carry a lightweight bicycle.

Armies often used bicycles as transportation. For example, the Japanese successfully used whole troops of bicyclists in the Malay Peninsula and Singapore, among other places in Asia. Thousands of Japanese soldiers bicycled along roads, down narrow paths, and along ***jungle*** trails to surround and defeat the British.

In Europe the German army sent bicycle troops ahead of their tanks to ***battle*** the Norwegian army. They knew that bikes could cross

---

行车解决了上述种种及其他问题。它不需要燃料，操纵起来安静容易。骑自行车者不需要正规路，他们能去许多卡车和坦克去不了的地方。或许最重要的是，士兵能轻松携带一辆重量轻的自行车。

军队经常使用自行车作为交通工具。例如，在马来半岛、新加坡以及亚洲其他地方，日本人成功地使用了整支自行车部队。成千上万的日本士兵骑着自行车，沿着道路、狭窄的小径和丛林小道，包围并打败了英国人。

在欧洲，德国军队派自行车部队先于他们的坦克跟挪威军队作战。他

---

jungle *n.* 丛林；密林

battle *v.* 与……作战

the ***steep*** Norway ***landscape*** more easily than tanks could. One night British soldiers ***parachuted*** into German-occupied France, quickly assembled bikes they had brought, and then sped silently away to destroy a radar station. Thus, this simple machine, the bicycle, was an important tool during World War II.

们知道自行车可以比坦克更容易穿越挪威陡峭的地形。一天晚上，英国士兵空降到德国占领的法国，很快组装起了他们带来的自行车，然后悄悄地急速驶去摧毁了一个雷达站。因此，自行车这个简单的机器在第二次世界大战期间是一个重要的工具。

---

steep *adj.* 陡峭的

landscape *n.* 地形；景观

parachute *v.* 空投；跳伞

38

The Conquests of Hernando Cortés

In 1519 Spanish explorer Hernando Cortés led an expedition to Mexico to gain land and gold for the Spanish Empire. Taking the route of an earlier explorer, Cortés sailed to the Yucatán. There he ***conquered*** the people of Tabasco. From them he learned about the wealthy Aztec Empire ruled by Montezuma. One of his

埃尔南·科尔特斯的征服

1519年，西班牙探险家埃尔南·科尔特斯率领一支探险队远征墨西哥为西班牙帝国获取土地和黄金。他沿着一名早期探险家的路线，向尤卡坦半岛驶去。在那里他征服了塔巴斯科居民。从他们那儿了解到了蒙提祖马统治下的富裕的阿兹特克帝国。他的

conquer *v.* 战胜；征服

captives, Malinche, knew both the Mayan and Aztec languages. Malinche became Cortés's interpreter and guide.

After sailing farther up the coast, Cortés landed and founded the first Spanish settlement in Mexico, today called Veracruz. There he met messengers from Montezuma, who brought Cortés gold and gifts. They also suggested that Cortés leave Mexico immediately. Cortés, however, was eager to capture the city from which such valuable gifts came, so he began his ***march*** inland to the Aztec capital, Tenochtitlán. Malinche had told Cortés about the many Native American peoples who disliked the Aztecs. Thus, along the way, Cortés formed an ***alliance*** with the Tlaxcalans, whom Montezuma had tried to conquer for many years.

一个俘虏，玛琳切，会玛雅语和阿兹特克语两种语言。玛琳切成了科尔特斯的翻译和向导。

在沿着海岸向上行驶了一段之后，科尔特斯靠了岸并在墨西哥建立了西班牙第一个殖民地，即今天的韦拉克鲁斯。在那里他遇到了蒙提祖马派来的信使，信使给他带来了黄金和礼物。他们同时建议科尔特斯立即离开墨西哥。然而，科尔特斯渴望夺得那些有珍贵礼物的城市，因此他开始向内陆的阿兹特克首都特诺奇提特兰城进军。玛琳切告诉科尔特斯很多印第安人不喜欢阿兹特克人。这样，沿途科尔特斯与特拉斯卡拉人形成了同盟，而蒙提祖马多年来一直想征服特拉斯卡拉人。

---

captive *n.* 囚徒；俘虏
march *n.* 行军；行进
alliance *n.* 同盟；联盟

Montezuma, meanwhile, listened to his messengers describe the appearance of the Spaniards and the ***odd*** weapon Cortés had fired. The Aztecs had never seen a gun, nor had they seen people on horseback. Montezuma thought that Cortés might be the god Quetzalcoatl, who had left earth long ago but was expected to return to ***claim*** his kingdom in 1519.

Although at first hesitant, Montezuma invited Cortés into the capital. There Cortés saw vast amounts of gold and other treasures. Afraid that the Aztecs would kill him and his forces, Cortés took Montezuma ***hostage***. While Cortés ruled the Aztecs through Montezuma, his forces melted gold to prepare it for shipment to Spain.

与此同时，蒙提祖马听取了信使对西班牙人的出现以及科尔特斯所用的古怪武器的描述。阿兹特克人从未见过枪，也没见过人骑马。蒙提祖马认为科尔特斯可能是羽蛇神，这些神灵很久以前离开地球但预计于1519年要回到他的王国。

尽管起初很犹豫，蒙提祖马还是邀请科尔特斯来到首都。科尔特斯见到了大量的黄金和其他财宝。因害怕阿兹特克人会杀了他和他的部队，科尔特斯把蒙提祖马扣为人质。当科尔特斯通过蒙提祖马统治阿兹特克人时，他的部队融化金子准备运回西班牙。

---

odd *adj.* 奇怪的；怪异的

claim *v.* 要求（拥有）；索取

hostage *n.* 人质

After a brief ***absence*** in the spring of 1520, Cortés returned to Tenochtitlán, where he found that the man he had left in charge had killed many Aztecs. The Aztecs attacked Cortés and his followers. Montezuma was killed during the battle, and most of Cortés's forces were killed as they tried to escape. Cortés and his remaining forces ***fled*** to Tlaxcala.

The next year, after gathering together many Native American allies, Cortés attacked Tenochtitlán. After several months, the last Aztec ruler surrendered. Cortés, continuing his conquests, explored parts of Central America and sent expeditions to conquer the rest of the Aztec Empire. Before long Cortés the conqueror had destroyed the Aztec Empire and claimed its lands for Spain.

在1520年春天科尔特斯暂时离开了特诺奇提特兰城，当他回来的时候，发现留下来负责的人杀了很多阿兹特克人。阿兹特克人攻击了科尔特斯和他的追随者。在战斗中蒙提祖马被杀死了，科尔特斯手下的大多数人在逃跑时也被杀死。科尔特斯和他剩下的部队逃到了特拉斯卡拉。

第二年，在聚集了许多印第安盟友后，科尔特斯袭击了特诺奇提特兰城。几个月之后，阿兹特克最后一位统治者投降。科尔特斯继续他的征服，对中美洲部分地区展开了探险，并派探险队征服阿兹特克帝国的其他地方。很快征服者科尔特斯摧毁了阿兹特克帝国，声称其土地归西班牙所有。

---

absence *n.* 缺席；不在

flee *v.* （尤指害怕有危险而）逃避；逃跑

39

The Mexican Flag and Its Symbolism

The current national flag of Mexico is similar to the one that was adopted in 1821 after Mexico won freedom from Spain. Both flags are ***tricolor*** with ***vertical*** stripes of green, white, and red. The three stripes are ***symbolic***, representing the "three guarantees", or "three promises", that Mexican leaders made to unite the people

墨西哥国旗及其象征意义

墨西哥现在的国旗与1821年其从西班牙赢得独立后所采用的相似。这两个国旗都是绿、白、红三种颜色的竖长条纹组成。这三个条纹具有象征意义，代表墨西哥领导人在争取从西班牙获得自由的斗争中所做出的团结人民的"三个保证"或"三个承诺"。绿色条纹象征独

tricolor *n.* 三色旗

vertical *adj.* 竖的；垂直的

symbolic *adj.* 使用象征的；作为象征的

in their struggle for freedom from Spain. The green stripe stands for independence, the white stripe for religion, and the red stripe for union.

The Mexican coat of arms appears on the white stripe. At times officials have ***altered*** the appearance of the coat of arms. It symbolizes the Aztec origins of Mexico City. According to legend, the Aztec god Huitzilopochtli directed the Aztecs to settle where they saw an eagle ***perched*** on a ***cactus***, eating a snake. In about 1325, the Aztecs found the place that Huitzilopochtli had described and began to build their capital city, Tenochtitlán.

On the earlier flag, a crowned eagle is standing on a cactus. On

---

立，白色象征宗教，红色象征统一。

墨西哥的国徽出现在白色部分。官方有时改变国徽的外观。它象征着墨西哥城来源于阿兹特克。根据传说，阿兹特克人的神灵太阳神指示他们在嘴叼着蛇的鹰站立的仙人掌所在地定居。大约在1325年，阿兹特克人找到了太阳神所描绘的地方，开始建造都城特诺奇提特兰城。

在早期的国旗上，一只头顶王冠的鹰站在仙人掌上。在今天的国旗

---

alter *v.* （使）改变；更改

perch *v.* （鸟）栖息；停留

cactus *n.* 仙人掌科植物

today's flag, an uncrowned eagle holding a snake is standing on a cactus. The cactus is growing from a rock surrounded by water, and a half circle of oak and *laurel* branches surrounds the bottom of the ***emblem***.

Thus, old or new, the national flags of Mexico represent similar ***historic*** events.

上，一只嘴里叼着蛇，头顶没有王冠的鹰站在仙人掌上。仙人掌从水中岩石里长出来，国徽下面由橡树和月桂枝组成的半环相托。

因此，无论是墨西哥旧国旗还是新国旗都描述相类似的历史事件。

---

laurel *n.* 月桂树

emblem *n.* 徽章；标记

historic *adj.* 历史上著名（或重要）的

40

Crossing the Threshold

Cultures have long known that human life tends to progress in stages—birth, childhood, adulthood, marriage, parenthood, and death. To mark the ***passage*** between these stages, people often conduct ***rituals*** called "***rites*** of passage". One such rite is for coming of age. This is the point at which childhood is

跨过门槛

不同文化长久以来就认为人的生命是分阶段前进的——这些阶段包括出生、童年、成年、结婚、成为父母和去世。为了记下这些阶段之间的转变，人们经常举行"人生大事及其庆祝典礼"这样的仪式。一个这样的仪式是为了纪念人成年。在这一刻，童年被认为已结束，

passage *n.* 章节；段落
ritual *n.* 仪式；礼节；程序
rite *n.* 仪式；典礼

thought to end and adulthood to begin. It has often been celebrated with complex community-wide rituals.

In today's Western world, modern customs have largely replaced such rituals. Getting a driver's license, attending a senior ***prom***, and graduating from high school are among the few coming-of-age ceremonies that many U.S. teenagers experience. However, some religions still provide young members with the ***option*** of taking part in a formal coming-of-age rite of passage.

A rite of passage has three main phases: separation, ***liminality***, and ***incorporation***. The three phases are marked by symbolic activities. In Roman Catholic Latin American cultures, many girls go through a ceremony called quinceañera on their fifteenth birthday. A special

---

而成年则刚开始。人们通常举行繁杂的、全民参与的仪式来庆祝。

在今日的西方世界，现代习俗很大程度上取代了这些仪式。获得驾驶证、参加毕业舞会和高中毕业，是许多美国青少年经历的为数不多的成人典礼。然而，一些宗教仍然为年轻的成员提供参加正式的成人礼的选择权。

成人礼有三个主要阶段：分离、阈限，以及融入。这三个阶段以一些象征性的活动为标志。在罗马天主教拉美文化中，许多女孩在15岁生日那天经历一个成人礼的仪式。一个特殊的弥撒确认女孩成为教堂的成年成

---

prom *n.* （尤指美国高中的）正式舞会
option *n.* 选择权；选择的自由
liminality *n.* 阈限
incorporation *n.* 结合；混合

Mass identifies the girl as an adult member of the church. During the reception that follows, the girl's father ***enacts*** his daughter's symbolic separation from childhood. He removes her flat shoes and places high-heeled shoes on her feet to symbolize her adulthood and readiness for ***courtship***.

The Amish have a unique way of acting out liminality in a coming-of-age ritual. Liminality is an in-between state in which people are not bound by the usual rules of their society. Among the Amish, ***baptism*** is celebrated in the late teen years. It represents a person's free choice to join the church as an adult. To prepare teenagers for this event, the Amish have a tradition called rumspringa, or "running around". During rumspringa, 16-year-olds are allowed to behave

---

员。在随后的招待会上，女孩的父亲表演他的女儿如何与童年象征性地分离。他脱掉她的平底鞋，帮她穿上高跟鞋，象征她已成年并为恋爱做好了准备。

阿曼门诺派在成人礼上有一套把阈限表现出来的独特方式。阈限是人们不受社会的一般规则约束的中间状态。在阿曼门诺派中，洗礼是在快20岁时举行的。它代表一个人作为成年人加入教会的自由选择。为了帮助青少年准备这个事，阿曼门诺派有一个传统，叫做“rumspringa”，或是“到处跑”。在这个传统期间，16岁的人被允许以阿曼门诺派正常禁止的

---

enact *v.* 扮演；担任……角色

courtship *n.* 求爱期；求爱；追求

baptism *n.* （基督教的）洗礼；浸礼

in ways that are normally forbidden by the Amish religion, such as attending parties, riding around in cars, and staying out late. The Amish believe that only after experiencing such activities can young people choose to give them up.

The ***bar mitzvah*** is another rite marking the beginning of religious adulthood. In a bar mitzvah rite, a 13-year-old Jewish boy signals his adulthood by leading his ***congregation*** in parts of the Sabbath service. The bar mitzvah is the public acknowledgment of a young man's new role in the Jewish faith. It helps to prepare him for the activities, rights, and duties that this role will ***entail***.

方式行事，例如参加宴会，开车到处跑，以及在外面待得很晚。阿曼门诺派相信年轻人只有经历过这些才能选择把自己交给上帝。

犹太男孩成人礼是另外一个标志宗教意义上成年开始的仪式。在犹太男孩成人礼上，13岁的犹太男孩通过在安息日仪式上带领祷告与诵经来表明其已成年。犹太男孩成人礼是对一个年轻人在犹太教信仰中的新角色的公开承认。这帮助他为这个角色所包含的活动、权利以及责任做好准备。

---

bar mitzvah 犹太男孩成人礼

congregation *n.* （教堂的）会众

entail *v.* 牵涉；需要；使必要

41

Happy Birthday, Sweet Fifteen!

The quinceañera, fifteenth-birthday celebration, is a special event in the lives of many girls of Latin American descent. A quinceañera can often be as ***elaborate*** as a wedding. The parents, with the help of ***sponsors***, buy the ***honoree***'s white or pastel dress. They order a cake and flowers, hire ***caterers***, buy gifts and party

生日快乐，甜蜜的15岁

庆祝15岁生日的成人礼，在许多拉美裔女孩的生活中是个特殊的事件。成人礼有时办得如同婚礼一样精致。在主办者的帮助下，父母为庆祝成人礼的女儿购买白色或色彩柔和的长裙。他们订购蛋糕和鲜花、雇人承办宴会、购买礼物和宴会小礼品、准备装饰品。他们还预定接待厅，安排音乐。参加成人礼的女孩选择一个主题，决定仪式上由谁

elaborate *adj.* 精心设计的

sponsor *n.* 主办者；赞助者

honoree *n.* 获奖人；领奖人

caterer *n.* 承办酒席的人；餐饮供应者

favors, and plan ***decorations***. They also reserve the reception hall and arrange for music. The girl selects a theme and chooses her ***escort*** and court of honor, which may include up to 14 couples.

The quinceañera generally begins with the misa de acción de gracias, or thanksgiving Mass, which marks the girl's ***commitment*** to Christian ideals. Afterward, the guests gather for a reception. A typical reception begins with the introduction of the honoree and the guests of honor. The girl's father or a male guardian then changes her shoes from flats to high heels. An honored female friend or relative places a ***tiara*** on her head. The girl may then give or receive a doll, symbolizing the last doll of her childhood. She and her father or guardian dance a waltz, which is followed by a rehearsed and choreographed dance performance by the entire court of honor. The parents or godparents offer a toast, the guests enjoy a traditional meal, and dancing and merrymaking continue until late.

来陪同她，挑选自己的伴舞团，伴舞团成员可能多达14对男女。

成人礼通常是以“misa de acción de gracias”或感恩弥撒开始的，这是女孩信奉基督教的标志。然后，客人们聚在一起参加招待会。一个典型的招待会以介绍庆祝成人礼本人和贵宾开始。接着女孩的父亲或是男性监护人把她的鞋由平底鞋换成高跟鞋。一名受人尊敬的女性朋友或亲人在她头上放一个冕状头饰。之后女孩可能会给出或收到一个玩具娃娃，象征着其童年最后的玩具。她和她的父亲或监护人跳一曲华尔兹，接着是整个伴舞团表演事先精心设计排练的舞蹈。父母或是教父教母来敬酒，客人们享受传统饮食，大家跳舞、尽情欢乐一直到很晚。

---

decoration *n.* 装饰品；装饰

commitment *n.* 信奉

escort *n.* （异性的）社交陪同

tiara *n.* 女式冕状头饰

42

Competition for Water in the American West

The American West is a large *region*. It stretches from the middle of North Dakota to the middle of Texas at its eastern edge, and it is bounded to the west by the Pacific Ocean. In this area, water is a very precious *resource*. The West receives an average of only 20 inches of *precipitation* per year—not enough to support farms or large

美国西部水资源之争

美国西部是一片巨大的区域。它的东部边缘从北达科他州延伸至德克萨斯州中部，西部以太平洋为界。在这一区域，水是非常宝贵的资源。西部年平均降水量只有20英寸——不足以维持农场或是大城

region *n.* 地区；范围
resource *n.* 资源；财力
precipitation *n.* （雨、雪、冰雹等的）降水量

cities. Also, the precipitation is not spread evenly through the region. For example, coastal Oregon and Washington receive a lot of rain, but many parts of the Southwest and California are deserts. These normally dry areas may receive ***bursts*** of heavy rain but then go for months with little or no rain.

This all-or-nothing nature of precipitation, along with rapid regional growth, makes it difficult to meet competing demands for water. Urban areas need water for homes, offices, shopping centers, and ***recreational*** uses. Big businesses—whether agricultural, mining, or manufacturing—require large amounts of water.

In the past, huge storage dams served as ***reservoirs*** to capture as much precipitation as possible. In addition, water was pumped from ancient natural underground pools called ***aquifers***. These earlier

---

市的用水。另外，这个地区降水量分布不均匀。例如，俄勒冈州海岸和华盛顿州雨水很多，但西南部和加利福尼亚州的许多地方却是沙漠。这些通常干燥的地方也许会有阵阵大雨，但接着几个月就会几乎没有雨。

这种全有或全无的降水量本质，加上地区的快速成长，很难满足人们对水的需求。城镇地区的家庭、办公室、购物中心以及娱乐都需要使用水。大的企业——无论是农业、矿业还是制造业——都需要大量的水。

在过去，巨大的蓄水坝充当水库来截留尽可能多的降水。此外，水从被称为含水层的古老天然地下水塘里抽出来。早期的解决方法引发了新问

---

burst *n.* 突出；迸发

reservoir *n.* 水库；蓄水池

recreational *adj.* 娱乐的；消遣的

aquifer *n.* （岩石或土壤的）含水层

solutions caused new problems. Overuse caused many aquifers to run dry. Building so many dams—blocking rivers and streams that once flowed freely—also has had harmful effects on the environment. For example, the dams prevent salmon from swimming upstream to their ***spawning*** grounds.

Traditionally, there have been two conflicting systems of water rights. The ***doctrine*** of ***riparian*** rights states that water belongs to all who own land along a river or other water source. The doctrine of appropriated rights states that water belongs to those who have first used the water, no matter how far away the water is.

Native Americans are a special group in the struggle for water rights. Until the 1960s, their claims to water rights on their lands were largely ignored. Now the courts are recognizing many of those claims.

题。过度使用造成许多含水层干涸。建造如此多的大坝——阻塞原本自由流动的河流小溪——对环境也有不良影响。例如，大坝阻止了大马哈鱼溯游而上回到其产卵之地。

传统上存在两种相冲突的水权制度。河岸权的信条是水属于临近河流或其他水源的土地所有者。而占有优先权的信条则是水属于首先使用的人，无论水有多远。

印第安人是水权争夺中的一个特殊群体。他们对自己土地上水权的主张很大程度上被忽略了，直到20世纪60年代。如今法院正承认这些主张。

---

spawn *v.* （鱼、蛙等）产卵

doctrine *n.* 教义；主义；学说；信条

riparian *adj.* 堤岸（上）的；堤岸近处的

New solutions include the idea of creating a water market where farmers might sell water rights on their land for urban use. Farmers would receive more money for selling water than for growing crops. Because an acre of urban land requires less water than an acre of ***irrigated*** farmland, more water would be available for cities. ***Conservation*** is another important strategy receiving attention. Ideas range from homeowners' using low-flow toilets and showerheads to manufacturers' recycling wastewater.

新的解决途径包括创建一个水市场，在这里农民可以出售自己土地上的水权供城市使用。农民出售水能获得比种庄稼更多的钱。因为一英亩的城市用地比起一英亩的灌溉农田需要更少的水，更多的水可供城市使用。节约是另一项正受到关注的重要策略。点子涵盖了从房主使用小流量马桶和花洒到制造商循环利用废水。

irrigate *v.* 灌溉　　**conservation** *n.* 防止流失；保持；保护

43

The Designer of Los Angeles's Water Supply

Born in 1855, William Mulholland rose from humble beginnings to become head of the Los Angeles Water Department. He began his career there as a *ditch* digger on the Los Angeles River. After work Mulholland taught himself *hydraulic* engineering. Within eight years, he was a *superintendent*.

洛杉矶供水系统设计者

威廉·穆赫兰生于1855年，他从低层的工作干起，后来成为了洛杉矶供水部门的负责人。他的工作生涯始于其在洛杉矶河上当一名挖沟人。下班后，他自学水力工程学。在8年的时间里，他成了主管。

ditch *n.* 沟渠　　**hydraulic** *adj.* 与水利系统有关的

superintendent *n.* 主管人；负责人

Knowing that the Los Angeles River would not be able to support the city's growing population, Mulholland looked to the larger Owens River, more than 200 miles away, as a source of water. He planned to build an ***aqueduct***—a combination of canals, tunnels, and pipelines—to carry the water from high in the Sierra Nevada across the desert to the city located near sea level.

First, he needed to ***procure*** land and water rights from the farmers in the Owens River Valley. The farmers had been hoping for a large federal ***irrigation*** project for their land. However, Mulholland convinced the government to support his plan instead. Through a combination of hard work and some politics, Los Angeles soon

---

穆赫兰知道洛杉矶河将无法养活城市不断增加的人口，他把二百多英里外的更大的欧文斯河看作是水源。他计划建一个引水渠——结合运河、隧道以及管道——把水从内华达山脉高处穿越沙漠运送到靠近海平面的城市。

首先，他需要从欧文斯谷农民那儿获得土地和用水权。农民们一直希望联邦政府为他们的土地修建一个大的灌溉工程。然而，穆赫兰说服政府反过来支持他的计划。通过努力以及一些政治手段，洛杉矶很快拥有了欧

---

aqueduct *n.* 渡槽；高架渠　　**procure** *v.* （设法）获得；取得；得到

irrigation *n.* 灌溉渠

owned the rights to most of the water in the valley.

The building of the aqueduct took more than five years. It was the largest American engineering project up to that time. Mulholland ***directed*** thousands of workers. In 1913 the people of Los Angeles received their first fresh water from the Owens River.

文斯谷大部分的水权。

引水渠的建设花了5年多的时间。它是到那时为止美国最大的工程项目。穆赫兰指挥着上千名工人。1913年，洛杉矶居民首次用上了来自欧文斯河的淡水。

---

direct *v.* 管理；监督；指导

The President's Cabinet

The members of the U.S. ***cabinet*** act as advisors to the president. They are the heads of the major departments of government. Most are given the title of "secretary". They serve at the pleasure of the chief ***executive***, although the Senate must approve their appointments. Unless they step down for some reason, they may

总统的内阁

政府主要部门的负责人作为美国内阁成员充当总统顾问。大多数内阁成员被授予"部长"的头衔。他们为行政长官即总统服务，虽然对其任命必须得到参议院的批准。除非因某种原因辞职，只要总

cabinet *n.* 内阁

executive *n.* 行政领导；领导层

hold their jobs for as long as the president is in office.

The cabinet has no direct control over changes in the law or decisions made by the government. How much power the members ***wield*** depends on their importance to the president. Some presidents prefer to seek advice from close personal ***associates*** rather than their cabinet appointees. On the other hand, some presidents have asked their most trusted friends to accept jobs in the cabinet.

George Washington named the members of the first cabinet in 1789. There were only four of them: the secretary of state, the secretary of the treasury, the secretary of war, and the ***attorney*** general. Over the years, as the country grew, managing this huge nation posed ever-greater challenges. The government met these

统在任他们就可以保留职位。

内阁无法直接控制法律修改或是政府决定。内阁成员具有多大的权力取决于其对总统的重要性。比起其任命的内阁成员，一些总统更喜欢向个人亲信寻求建议。另一方面，一些总统让其最可信赖的朋友接受内阁职位。

1789年乔治·华盛顿任命了首届内阁成员。一共只有四人：国务卿、财政部长、战争部长和司法部长。多年来，随着国家的成长，管理这一庞大的国家有了比以往任何时候更大的挑战。政府在某种程度上通过增

wield *v.* 拥有；运用；行使；支配

associate *n.* 同事；伙伴

attorney *n.* （业务或法律事务上的）代理人

challenges, in part, by increasing the size of the cabinet. The first secretary of the ***interior***, for instance, was named in 1849. This person oversees the country's natural resources, national parks, and historic sites. Since 1903, the secretary of ***commerce*** has focused on domestic business matters as well as trade with foreign countries.

The composition of the cabinet can reflect current concerns of the American people. In 2002, for instance, the year after attacks on Washington, D.C., and New York City, Congress enacted ***legislation*** to create the Department of Homeland Security. The new agency takes over responsibilities from some other departments and oversees new projects. Similar changes have occurred in the past, when large

---

加内阁规模来迎接这些挑战。例如，1849年任命了第一任内政部长。其负责管理全国的自然资源、国家公园以及历史遗址。自1903年以来，商务部长便专注于国内和对外贸易。

内阁构成能够反映美国人民当前的关注热点。例如，在2002年，也就是华盛顿特区和纽约市遭到袭击后的一年，国会颁布法律创设国土安全部。这一新机构接管其他一些部门的职责，监督新项目。类似的变化也

---

interior *n.* 内政；内务

commerce *n.* 贸易；商业；商务

legislation *n.* 法律；法规

departments have been broken into smaller ones. In the year 2002, the cabinet had 15 members.

All members are supposed to have equal ***status***. Two positions, however, can exert great influence in government. One is that of ***attorney general***. As the country's "top lawyer" and head of the Department of Justice, this person is often one of the most visible members of the cabinet. The secretary of state also has a high public profile and is considered the chief cabinet member. This person must work closely with the president on a day-to-day basis to build good relations with other nations.

出现在了过去大部门被分解成较小部门的时候。2002年，内阁有15名成员。

所有成员一般被认为是地位平等的。然而，两个职位在政府里具有重大影响力。一个是司法部长职位，作为国家的“首席律师”以及司法部的负责人，其经常是内阁里最引人瞩目的成员之一。国务卿同样受公众注目，并被认为是主要的内阁成员。其必须每日与总统一起密切工作，跟其他国家建立起良好的关系。

---

status *n.* 法律地位（或身份）　　**attorney general** 司法部长